OUT OF THE

OZARKS

William Childress

Southern Illinois University Press

Carbondale and Edwardsville

Copyright © 1987 by William Childress
Printed in the United States of America

Edited by Curtis L. Clark

Designed by Richard Hendel

Production supervised by Natalia Nadraga

Library of Congress Cataloging-in-Publication Data

Childress, William.

  Out of the Ozarks.

  1. Ozark Mountain Region.   I. Title.

F417.09C47   1987   976.7′1   87-4609

ISBN 0-8093-1365-0

ISBN 0-8093-1366-9 (pbk.)

90 89 88 87   5 4 3 2

The paper used in this publication meets the minimum requirements of
American National Standard for Information Sciences—Permanence of Paper
for Printed Library Materials, ANSI Z39.48-1984. ∞™

Contents

🌺 🌺 🌺

Preface

I was born along the Oklahoma edge of the Ozarks but left as a child. Many years later, world traveled and weary, I came back to live here. That was April 1974, and I've been here ever since. I have now lived in the Ozarks longer than I have ever lived anywhere else. I have traveled all over the world, yet nowhere have I found the mixture of natural beauty, wilderness, and quaint but rigorous life-style so evident in these hills.

Though humans have lived in the Ozarks for ten thousand years, this fifty-five thousand square miles of rugged and lovely landscape remains, for many, an enigma wrapped in a riddle. Eons ago the Ozarks were as high as the Himalayas—but wind, rain, and glaciers have worn them down like an old mule's teeth. Once among the most awesome mountains on the planet, today their highest point—in Arkansas's Boston Mountains, within the Ozark range—measures only 2,578 feet. Formed by ancient sea beds, these gently rolling hills now rest on a vast plateau that touches seven states: Oklahoma, Kansas, Missouri, Illinois, Kentucky, Tennessee, and Arkansas.

The Ozarks begin in Illinois and Kentucky and stretch across two states to almost touch Tulsa, Oklahoma. Five major rivers (the Mississippi, the Osage, the Missouri, the Neosho, and the Arkansas) form their boundaries, and there are more free-flowing streams here than anywhere else in the United States. And the limestone nature of the soil makes possible other wonders—a vast number of bubbling fresh springs and more caves (at least seven thousand are now known) than any other place in the world. Crystal springs by the hundreds pour from tumbled landscapes after torrential rains. Some, like Bennett Spring, near Lebanon, Missouri, foam forth as much as one hundred million gallons of water a day. Near Fifty-Six, Arkansas, Blanchard Springs Caverns features both a beautiful spring and an equally beautiful cave (operated for vacationers by the U.S. government since 1972).

There is no place on earth to match this area, but the pioneer lifestyles that still exist off the main roads and back in the hills are not for everyone—one California couple I knew lasted six weeks before heading back west. The pace of life here is as slow as the traffic on the winding, two-lane highways. (If speed is your specialty, don't drive in the Ozarks. Mountain roads are unforgiving.)

The Ozarks, in fact, are for something almost lost to fast-paced Americans—the slow, enjoyable sipping of sights, sounds, and scenery. Late April finds hills tapestried with white dogwoods and pink redbud trees, while the earth sparkles with a million floral jewels: verbena, goldenrod, jack-in-the-pulpit, tiger lily, wild roses, and wild sweet william. I even love the old cemeteries here, some well-kept, some abandoned. A favorite is the grand and ancient one in Hermann, Missouri, where tombstones 150 years old spill down a green hillside or are gripped by the gnarled roots of great cedar trees. And there is nothing to compare to the silence that falls with the sun, which deepens as dusk deepens, and which is quietest in the dark, star-splintered night. (Ozarkians like it quiet enough to talk to god without shouting, which they often do. If you come here without a religion, any number of folks will offer one.)

In writing my newspaper column for the *St. Louis Post-Dispatch* over a period of the last four and a half years, I've traveled many an Ozark byroad and hiked many a trail. Yes, this is cattle country, horse country complete with mounted posses for escaped convicts, and above all, chicken country (hens in Arkansas and Missouri produce a billion eggs a month); but towns, little and large, are also part of the mosaic of these mountains. Towns such as Anderson, Pineville, Goodman, Lanagan, Noel, Rocky Comfort, Powell, Bethpage, and Jane—all in my own McDonald County—often appear, to the first-time visitor, to be crumbling and headed for oblivion, but behind the old brick walls and faded nineteenth-century facades, these tiny hamlets guard their secrets. See these towns as you wish to. It's your loss if you don't look deeper, to the character of the hardy French, German, and Scots-Irish who settled these hills as long ago as 1735.

As a writer, I've always felt the people make the place. But here, the place also shapes the people. McDonald County, according to the ivory domes at Harvard, is one of the ten poorest counties in the nation. Maybe, but we're not poor in pride. I see folks fail in business, and the very next month it seems like they're back with some other business. We have our bums and parasites, like everyplace, but the work ethic is alive and well in the Ozarks. In my little town of Anderson, folks often hold down more than one job. Everybody in a family who can work, works. We are survivors.

We know what we've got and treasure it, but the Ozarks are changing, too. You don't have to like change—it just comes. I've gone "turtlin'" in Missouri marshes with the late "Turtle" Ivy, bringing back alligator snappers for a succulent turtle fry, but Earl's gone now and I don't know any more turtle catchers. Creek-bank fish fries used to be numerous, and attract hundreds, and maybe a local country or bluegrass group would show with guitars and fiddles a-bristle (there's nothing like mountain music—still a favorite in the Ozarks—to recall a simpler, sweeter time), but the last fry I went to was five years ago. And not far from Anderson is Sulphur Springs, Arkansas, once famed for its mineral waters and baths. A rerouted highway ruined its tourist trade, though once it was the destination of trains filled with excursionists who came to "take the waters." (Not all came for that purpose. Trains once brought soldiers to fight. I've been to Pea Ridge Battlefield, now a national park, many times. Arkansas's War Eagle Mills was also a battleground. As a friend of mine who collects arrowheads says, "This part of the Ozarks ranges historically from flint knives to Civil War cannonballs.")

Folks live in the Ozarks because—like the sign in Bella Vista, Arkansas, labeled "Suits-Us Drive" suggests—it suits them. Making a living here is hard, but living here is easy. As my longtime neighbor Kenny Shaver says, "I was born and raised in these hills, but once, to make a living, I had to go to Kansas City. I had to get used to fear and crime and the crazy pace of city life, and me and my wife Lucy swore we'd save every penny towards the day we could buy some land and move back down here forever."

"The way I see it," Kenny once told me, "is that I owe my family first, my neighbors next, and my county, state, and country next. I figger it makes sense to stack 'em like that—in order of importance to me. I figger if I take care of me and mine, the world will take care of it."

When you get right down to it, that's not a bad philosophy.

Acknowledgments

First and foremost, I gratefully acknowledge the *St. Louis Post-Dispatch* (a publication of the Pulitzer Publishing Company), in which seventy-one of the eighty-six columns and articles collected in this book appeared between 1982 and 1987.

The other columns and articles collected here first appeared in *Friends, Sports Afield, TV Guide, McCalls, Writer's Digest, Texas Flyer, Ford Times, Country Roads,* and *Country Living.* I'm grateful to the editors and publishers of these fine magazines for their consideration of my work over the years.

Prologue

He spent his childhood hours in a den
of rushes, watching the gray rain braille
the surface of the river. Concealed
from the outside world, nestled within,
he was safe from parents, God, and eyes
that looked upon him accusingly,
as though to say: Even at your age,
you could do better. His camouflage
was scant but it served, and at evening,
when fireflies burned holes into heaven,
he took a path homeward in the dark,
a small Noah, leaving his safe ark.

Sometimes when the shadows lengthen across the fields and the sun seems to gaze from the horizon like a kindly eye, the walnut grove becomes my temple. Here the heretic comes, sans book, sans prayer, to talk with forest sprites and dream of elves.

Not for this place the plans of men, the crowded stones of cities. This is sanctuary, my sacred Vale of Tempe, a place dedicated to the worship of dreams. "Life is but a dream," the old song goes, and there is more to that than we want to believe. How often I stop what I am doing to think back over the clock-ticks that have passed into the vast river of no return.

Already I turn on the axle of my years; already I creak in little ways—for the oil of youth is quickly drying. Am I missing anything on my journey? Some kiss, some blow, some word of kindness or anger? It's all part of it. To miss anything life has to offer is, for me, a piece of death.

I throw my arms around a tree in the gathering dusk, put my ear to its heart, listen for the running of its blood. I know all the old tales. The spirits, always lovely and feminine, in the wood; the shy eyes peeping that I'll never see. In the green gowns of their leaves, swaying in the pre-storm wind, the trees do seem so like dancing maidens. If it is imagination's warp that weaves the spell, I don't care.

I know other groves, other dark caverns of trees—some with tombstones guarding the bones of old pioneers who had the grace of good fortune to be buried where they wished. Law, that wrangling rooster-pit of equity for all, decrees that the dead can no longer be buried in such places. There are cities for the dead. Put them there.

Sometimes I sit for hours, trying to call forth in phrases that body from the ground, that spirit which once strolled this American earth—that lived, fought, loved, cursed, died; that sought God, and found him or not; that dreamed of justice and knew injustice; that saw unworthy men rewarded and good men ignored; that scaled the pyramid of years and descended to oblivion.

The storm is coming closer, crossing the Great Plains, the imaginary lines and man-made names—South Dakota, Nebraska, Kansas,

Oklahoma—winds that swept here when the only lines were the ruts of buffalo trails.

I think the trees are magnets for the winds, that they meet and join in a dance that fuses ontology with cosmology, being with grace, the latter some universal force we long to recognize and can't—yet brazen with names anyhow. How loudly we cry "Come down, God," "Show your face, Allah," "Smile at me, Buddha." If we can see the wind, we can see them.

To all of those whose inner being seems empty, I recommend a sojourn in the forest of their choice. A solitary walk, for you may want to talk to those who do not answer—and someone with you might not know that muteness, too, serves a purpose. "Study to be quiet," says Izaak Walton, that great fisherman, in the stained glass window of the chapel by Westminster Abbey, though he owes it to a much older source.

The deepening amber of the sun sends fingers of fire through the trees, copper-gold bands creating bars of light and darkness. Out, out across the pasture, fading and dying as the sun vanishes, out towards the sassafras trees, the Grove of Dancing Maidens, out to the edge of the far eastern woods, past the scattered cows who crop the thick grass and pay night's forward march no mind.

The clouds boil thick and black in the north. The wind has died. The walnut trees are still. I raise the atoms of the dust I will become and go inside.

1

There is a golden circle in the sky,
perhaps the pale halo
of some wandering angel,
who looks down on earth and whispers,
"How strange."

The gold descends like a coverlet,
cloaking a meadow where horses graze,
their legs like stalks
in the yellow grass.

The light shifts
as it does in the forest,
making hazy pillars
that lean against darkness
like the bones of some dead city.

Sky of indigo, of velvet,
there are weavers at work.
The king of needles is stitching the night
into a tapestry for the midnight sun.

Iwas asleep and dreaming, an odd dream echo-
ing with shouts and movement. The shouts
drew nearer, and suddenly I was thrown from
my bed to land with a thump on the hard plank floor of the shack we
lived in. It was April 21, 1940—midnight in a Phoenix, Arizona, slum.

"Get up, Son, get up!" a voice screamed in my ear. "The house is
on fire!"

I opened my eyes. Mom stood over me in a pink nightslip, her eyes
bulging with terror as she dragged me to my feet. Under her right
arm, held like a squirming sack of grain, was my infant sister. Orange
flames lapped like waves across the ceiling.

The next thing I knew, I was slapped awake and being hauled pell-
mell toward the door. Mom's hair was on fire, but she did not stop.
She made a wild rush at the plywood door that divided the blackness
outside from the brightness within.

Now her tattered old nightslip was smoking around the edges. She
did not stop to beat out the fire because too many bigger flames were
roaring and snapping around us. Rich yellow juice oozed from the
shack's cheap pine boards, feeding the inferno.

The door cracked under Mom's 180 pounds, but in spite of the
rusty hinges that had always looked ready to fall off, it held. Mom
screamed, "We've got to get out of here!" and smashed into the door
again, full force. This time she won. With her two shrieking kids, she
sprawled in the dooryard—directly in front of two men plying a garden hose.

"We never knew nobody was in there!" one of the men yelled.
They turned the hose on us, putting out Mom's hair and soothing
the pain from her burns for a moment.

Mom's hair was singed to the roots in places. My baby sister was
unhurt, and all I had was a couple of skinned places from skidding on
the ground. I was seven years old—and all the years that have come
to me since have been mine because of my mother's actions.

The fire consumed our two-room shack, four bungalows, several
homemade house trailers and some smaller buildings. It turned out
to be arson; the fire was set by the woman who owned the slum so
she could collect the fire insurance. She died in prison.

My mother was a hero that night, but nobody noticed. And I have the feeling that most real heroes never are noticed. Not for them the fanfare and accolades of a grateful public. Not for them the scrolls and medals, trophies of society's gratitude.

The real heroes I'm talking about are "just folks"—people trying to get through one more day with their spirits and families intact. The real heroes are the mothers and fathers of all of us. Yet a lot of them, in their old age, are finding that their country is letting them down. And in many cases, so are their kids—the children they gave birth to, nourished, protected, and worried about for all the years it took to bring them safely to adulthood.

It seems a part of the human riddle that we never appreciate what we can take for granted. Our parents are "just there," for those times when we need them. And mostly, we wish we didn't need them at all—because after all, when we are growing up, it is obvious to everyone but our parents that we know more than they do.

When we are kids, two things are uppermost in our minds—fun and food. I once calculated that I owe my parents for approximately 34,200 pounds of groceries for the years one through eighteen—at which point the U.S. Army took over my care and feeding. If they ever decide to call in the debt, it will bankrupt me. And yet, not long ago, some fool kid actually tried to sue his parents for not giving him a more luxurious life.

Our family lived poorly, but we lived. Poverty is something you notice most when you look back on it. We never had a lot of cake to eat, but we always had biscuits. And although the years of unremitting toil took their toll on my parents, those years also made them durable—as their current ages show. It is unlikely that today's underworked, overweight generation of Americans will set longevity records.

Often, our only toys were slabs of old linoleum on a grassy hill, but I betcha we had more fun then than most kids do today with their fancy electronic toys.

My parents and I have often disagreed, especially when I was a teenager and they tried to tell me they knew more than I did. But as I've grown older, and especially since I've become a parent, I have come to appreciate the years and dollars they spent raising me. Our paths have sometimes been on opposite sides of the world, but my parents have always been with me.

✿✿ ✿✿ ✿✿

I live in the Ozarks, where we treasure simple virtues. Virtues like settin', just plain settin', in a chair, leaned back on a porch, watchin'.

There are few arts left to the common man that require such simple equipment, so little preparation, and so modest an outlay of energy. Settin', not horse racin', should be the sport of kings.

The humble hills where I live and do some settin' boast the world's finest practitioners of this fading art. Except for a few phonies in hillbilly movies, we may be the last. But don't ever tell an Ozarkian "You people sure do a lot of sitting around here."

First, no one will understand your strange way of talking, and you'll be marked as an outsider. Outsiders can't set, and they don't talk right, either. Second, your concern with time means you're in a hurry—in which case you never should have come to the Ozarks in the first place. Settin' and talkin' are done without any clocks.

You must never say "sitting." You should only say "settin'." "Sitting" calls forth all that is prim, proper, and a pain in the neck. But "settin'"? "Settin'" means tilted-back chairs, lazy talk, and solid comfort. Settin' is the *ne plus ultra* of relaxation, often following a dinner of fried squirrel, cornbread, grits, and fresh churned buttermilk. It can be the setting for a political discussion, but only if everyone agrees.

"That politician shore pulled th' wool over our eyes."

"Ah agree."

"So do Ah."

No one knows who first invented settin'. Or who went on and refined it to its present perfection. I learned from an uncle who lived in a little town outside of Kansas City. Tall and lanky, he wrung admiration from us urchins because, no matter how slick the porch planks were, he never once fell from his tilted-back position.

His spiderlike legs prevented it. If he started to lose control, one or the other of his lanky legs would swing back and prop him up till he got his balance back. Not everyone could do this, and the clatter of a chair followed by the thump of a body made for real porch music, especially among young men just learning how to set.

Also, Uncle Tom was the only man I ever knew who could smoke and chew tobacco at the same time. If his Bull Durham butt went out, he took it right in with his Micky Twist chaw so as not to waste it. He remained a champion setter right up until the day tobacco killed him.

Settin' is Southern in origin and rural in execution. City folks can't practice it because they don't have porches. Porches and settin' go together like hounds and huntin'.

Not that it's a seasonal art, exactly. Except for winter, it's a year-round pursuit. And if you get rained off the porch, you can always move indoors—although the womenfolk keep a sharp eye on leanin' back, because the chairs might rip the wallpaper. "I've only had that wallpaper forty years," I've heard my aunt tell my uncle grimly, "and I ain't about to replace it now."

If you're under sixteen, moving indoors is done as though the chair is part of your bottom—by reaching underneath it and snugging it up against your rump.

If you're over sixteen, you're much too impressed with yourself for kid stuff like that, and so you try the adult method—which may not always work. Adults simply turn to any handy urchin and growl, "Brang 'at chair in yere." Over-sixteens who say this can get a knot on their shin.

Chairs for settin' can be many and varied. In an emergency—such as company comin'—logs, stumps, or upturned buckets can be pressed into service. But these rustic replacements automatically preclude tiltin'—about which more in a minute. The chairs most preferred are called straightback or kitchen chairs. In general they have stout hickory legs and backs like small ladders. Bottoms are woven of green willow wands or caned, but if these wear out any handy board can be nailed on as a seat—a practice that makes strong antique dealers weep.

Rocking chairs are all right for settin', but they're generally the choice of women. Women don't give a fig for tiltin'. Tiltin' is a man's game, and young men see it as a mark of manhood—like chawin' and spittin'. (Not everyone lasts at these latter arts, especially if a chum whacks them on the back while they're tilted back chawin'. Mickey Twist has ruined lots of digestions, but kept many a boy from the tobacco-stained path.)

Since they take terrible punishment, only the strongest chairs are suitable for tiltin'. If you make even the slightest miscalculation, you're suddenly flailing the air to get your balance—and if the chair doesn't splinter under you you're embarrassed anyway, especially if experts are watching.

The idea is to ease back just enough so that your chair thumps against the wall, leaving you cocked at a thirty-degree angle. This is a sinfully comfortable pose, and one orthopedists deplore. More than a thirty-degree slant is perilous, but a few daredevils just out of puberty still risk being maimed as they inch and creak towards the fatal forty-five.

As an art, which is what it is, settin' is civilized to the point of placidity. Peaceful is the heart, tranquil is the mind of the veteran setter. With years of experience behind him, he has little to do but enjoy his eminent position and evict another family of sparrows from the porch rafters with the smoke from his corncob pipe. (Mickey Twist is on a par with cats for bird eviction.)

A truly skilled setter is often musically inclined, blowing a french harp ("frainch harp") or rolled-up leaf while tapping time with his toes on the hound at his feet. (I have done that many a time, and I'm here to tell you hounds don't give splinters.) If company should show up, he just drawls, "Yall drag up a cheer an' set awhile."

"Why, much a-bliged," they say. "Cain't stay long, though."

Out come the tin-can cuspidors and plugs of Mickey Twist, and the spittin' begins, *spang, spang, spang.* Spittin' is an art in the Ozarks, too, but that must wait for another time.

❀ ❀ ❀

One of my favorite aunts was named Thelma. She was a tall, seemingly austere woman with auburn hair and brown eyes. But she wasn't what she seemed at all, for mostly Thelma took what life dished out and still came back for more.

She never had time for much besides being a wife and mother—especially the latter, for four daughters and five sons were born to her. I only got to see her when our families got together—a long ride from the middle to the edge of the state. But every so often, I would get lucky and catch her without a lot of others, or even her kids, bothering her. That was when I bothered her.

"Aunt Thelma," I asked her once, "what's death?"

"It's when you leave this earth and go to live somewheres else, like heaven."

And when I asked where heaven was, she gave my favorite answer to this day: "It's out yonder someplace."

She answered with a wide sweep of her hand, which was often coated with flour and left a fine white dust in the air. I knew immediately what she meant. Heaven was out near the north forty.

Eight is as good an age as any to go looking for heaven, especially when you've just been given such good instructions. The north forty lay down by Cache Creek, a pecan-treed branch that normally held some clear pools along its graveled course. Naturally, you don't undertake so serious a journey without provisions. I asked for some biscuits and a little bacon grease to put on them.

"Whatever for, child?"

"I figgered maybe I'd go take a look for heaven," I told her seriously. "I ain't never seen none o' them angels folks keep talkin' about, and it's about time I got acquainted with one."

The north forty was the best land on the place, creek bottom that caught all the rich nutrients that washed downstream during spring rains. Tall pecans, oaks, and elms sentried the banks. It was a mighty pretty place, but after all, heaven was supposed to be a better country.

This wasn't bad country, but even though my uncle raised watermelons and cotton here, I'd seen better. The search soon made me hungry, so I found a quiet pool down in the creek and tore into the biscuits. The water was dark but clear, but it hadn't rained in a while. I found where the water trickled for a distance over gravel and got a drink to wash down the grease and biscuits. But it didn't look to me as if I was any closer to heaven then when I'd started out.

Squatting by the creek, I saw several dragonflies dancing just above the water. Two were connected somehow, tail to head. Their shimmering wings might have been gossamer—which I bet anything was a heavenly ingredient of some sort.

They paid me no mind, just went on skimming, dancing, and zipping backward and forward with the speed of light. And suddenly the water boiled and up shot the biggest bass I ever saw and put an end to the bug ballet.

I never did find heaven that day, though I got close enough, as far as I was concerned, when I stumbled on a big old watermelon twined among the young cottonstalks. I "plugged" it with my Case pocket-knife. It was perfect, and I liked to've broke a gut on just the heart-meat before I finally got some sense and staggered homeward, picking occasional wildflowers on the way.

"Did you find heaven?" Aunt Thelma smiled as I walked in the door and gave her my white-rag lunchbucket and sweaty bouquet.

"No ma'am," I said. "But I mighta seen a couple of angels make dinner for a bass."

Years, and life, and the endless battles between saints, sinners, evangelists, sects, and religions have made me pretty much of a Doubting Thomas in the matter of heaven. If an eight-year-old kid can't find it, who can? But maybe the answer for all of us lies in our final apartment—the smallest we'll ever dwell in.

Out yonder someplace.

❀ ❀ ❀

Like fishes suspended in water, we swim through our days. It is that nebulous time of year in the Ozarks when we inhabit clouds that have forgotten their proper place in the sky and have come down to wrap us in a wet grayness. We're cheered only by the nearness of spring.

On the biggest walnut tree in my front yard there is an old cow skull that I picked up years ago in the northeast pasture. I brought it to the trailer, painted "Welcome" jaggedly across its forehead, and spiked it to the tree. It's better than a Wal-Mart welcome mat. The cow—who loved attention and died my first year here—probably would appreciate it.

We are all hopeful that spring is here, even this early—as the groundhogs have promised. Even if they didn't see their shadows, they still remain down under. Their waddly forms won't be around for several weeks yet.

When Groundhog Day came and went, I paid it the same amused attention most folks do—the same attention I also pay to weather forecasters. Years ago, in London during winter (it's wet and gray, much like our hill weather here), I said something to the girl I was with about our custom of watching marmots come out of their holes as augurs of spring. She told me that their Candlemas (also February 2) did the same for them and recited a little verse: "If Candlemas be fair and bright / Winter will have another flight / But if the day brings clouds and rain / Winter will not come again."

Alas, I parted from my pretty to return to my Army unit across the channel. In my absence, spring came, bringing with it a new swain—and a Dear John letter for me. Groundhogs, indeed! Let them keep their noses out of the weather.

A swarm of fat raindrops rattles against the side of my study and on the trailer roof. By the door that leads into this add-on room, the same dark stain marks the invasion of water that has gathered on the crude patio I built years ago. I accidentally sloped the concrete floor inward and have paid a wet price every rain since.

Water glissades down the window panes like mineral oil. A solitary bird—a jay, naturally—perches briefly on the skull, cocks his head and peers into the eyes of death, then spots my movements at the typewriter and zips away.

The black limbs with their hanging vines seem to clutch the haze, bringing it closer. Humidity is near saturation point now, dripping from every eave, shed, and limb. The earth smells like a cave and is the muddiest I've ever seen it.

How long it takes such surface saturation to reach the water table is anyone's guess; my guess is it takes a long time. In summer, Ozark rains penetrate the rocky soil as though striking screen wire. But in winter, the ground must be frozen deep below, for seepage is slow.

Enough!

Surely, there is cheer to be had somewhere. Ah! There it is, in the 18-by-36-inch fluorescent light set flat in my study ceiling. At least a hundred wasps lie inside it, their dark shapes caught between the light and the plastic cover. It's cheering to know that they, at least, won't be crawling out of every cranny when the weather gets warm. I filled the entire space with waspicide last fall.

Of course, I never got them all, but dodging them will add energy to my days—and they are the best harbinger of spring I know of. Each one of the little beggars carries its own alarm clock, and I've never known a wasp to be late for an appointment.

Sometimes, when I see yet another educational television show about the balance of nature, I scoff because I'm certain any intelligence, natural or otherwise, messed up by inventing wasps. I have never met one that I gave a hang about, but some have liked me well enough to kiss me on the first meeting. Talk about a fiery passion.

Wasps—especially the big ones down here—can sting as many times as they've a mind to, and still go out for lunch. Bees, which hurt less, can sting only once and end up at a funeral. It's not fair.

So our war on the wasps, and theirs on us, finds a truce only in the wintertime—when they're either snoozing or, as in my case, have been permanently nixed.

If I open my study door, will a wall of water rush in? Well, these walls full of maps, notes, rejection slips, and family pictures are closing in. I'm for the outdoors, foggy or not.

As always when he is near enough to see my door open, a little black pooch *rarfs*! and bangs against it. Up he jumps, muddy paws streaking my jeans. He's begging to be chased, to be bowled over, to be told in various ways that winter is dead, and it's time to start living again. I grin in spite of the gray day.

🌸 🌸 🌸

They had parlors when I was a kid, but of course they weren't found in sharecroppers' shacks—although it was not uncommon for my late Uncle Tom Childress to say "I'm going to the parlor" as he headed out back.

I got to go in a parlor once. Dad had had some dealings with the rich cotton grower we were working for, and we had to go to "the big house." This one sat on a hill, where cyclones could hit it more easily but never did, preferring the poor shacks below, as did the floods. God may not love the rich, but he doesn't hate them either.

First off, the rich farmer talked the way we did. He pronounced parlor "porler." "Less go own in th' porler," he announced in his East Texas accent. So Dad followed him into the porler. And his fat kid, the usual sneer on his puss, half shoved me into the porler, too—mostly with his belly. I hated that kid. He wasn't worth a dirty handkerchief. And on a future day he would get me in trouble, and I would whip him for it, then get whipped myself by Dad because I jumped on the boss's kid.

"But dang it, Pa, he's *bigger'n* me!" I yelled as I hopped.

"Then you shoulda run," Dad replied, "and made the little whelp feel good."

Dad didn't really lay on, and in his homely way he was teaching a lesson that everyone must learn: Life isn't fair, and you gotta get along, little dogie. With a family of six to feed, he couldn't afford the luxury of offending the grower who paid us—no matter how meager the coin. Authority isn't always right, but it is always authority.

In the porler on that day, Dad and Mr. English talked about "second pickings." This is gleaning, pure and simple, and a big pain in the back because you get less cotton, hence make less money. But Mr. English flattered Dad, saying as how his family made quite a crew, and that he was willing to raise the per-pound price some if we would stay on after most of the other pickers left.

That's about all I got out of it, though, because I was goggling that porler pretty good. Of course the kid was watching me, much like a street cop eyes a known thief, and I longed to paste him. He sidled up to me and said, "I betcha ain't seen a real Victrola before."

Sure enough, a shiny upright record player with a big bell horn stood in a corner. "That cost more money'n your folks make in a month," he sneered—but not so his father could hear him. I expect Mr. English didn't know what his kid was really like and might have taken him to another kind of porler if he had.

There was also an overstuffed sofa, a chair or two, a flag on a pole, and a desk with drawers. It looked spiffy enough to me, but I've been in lots better porlers since—not as a cotton picker but as a teacher. (Come to think of it, those two professions might be related. My back hurt when I was a teacher, too.)

I grew up believing that a parlor was some swank place where ladies sat around sipping tea and talking. Years later, I looked at a dictionary and found out that my kinfolks were pretty much on target. Because I knew how to shine, even at that early age, I got my two favorite cousins, Jimmy and Johnny, and educated them.

"I reckon you don't know what a porler is?" I said to them.

"Why, shore," Jimmy said instantly. "They's one in the Dutchman's house across the crick."

"But do you know what it *means*?" I said, eyeing them dead-on.

"Shore do," Johnny chimed in. "It means he's got more money'n we have."

"It means," I said, ignoring Johnny, "to *talk*. It comes from the French word *parler,* and . . ."

"Huh," Jimmy said thoughtfully. "Reckon that's right, Billy. I walked past that beauty porler they got in town and I never heered so much talkin' in my life. They wasn't talkin' French, though. They was talkin' just like us."

You're not going to straighten out some folks' thinking no matter how hard you try, so I gave up on my cousins. To this day, they probably think a beauty parlor is a place where women go to talk instead of to get their hair done.

I found out there was another kind of parlor when I got in the Army. This was the "parlor car" on trains fitted out for soldiers. Uncle Sam saw no reason to waste money on Pullmans for us GIs, so we sat in seats in parlor cars until we either reached our destination or died, whichever was first or cheaper. Those were the days when the Pentagon was actually told how much it could spend, and it spent that much and no more.

Pretty primitive times.

❋ ❋ ❋

This winter's hangin' on like a dog to a bone."

Big Al Schlueter owns a whitewashed building on the curve just past the railroad underpass as you come into Anderson, Missouri. In more genteel times, when any sort of drinking was glared on by the local good folks, the place was called Al's Tobacco Shop. Then cancer came along, and tobacco was out. Booze, though still disreputable, didn't cause cancer of the lungs, so today it's Al's Liquor Store.

"I bet it ain't rained this much in the whole *history* of this place," says Big Al. "What's it been, twelve straight days now?"

It's been nearly that. April has come in with webbed feet. The earth is a sodden sponge, and water runs in rivulets down each ditch and digs runnels in the dirt roads that graders will have to repair later.

On the picturesque cliffs flanking Missouri Route 59, which runs from Anderson to Noel, small waterfalls have erupted—a sure sign of an overburdened earth. But the cliffs are layered sandstone, and mudslides are rare.

The drive to Noel is one of the prettiest in the area. Anderson first, then Lanagan, then Ginger Blue and finally Noel—"The Christmas

City." Each December, a tree anchored in the Elk River, which runs by the town, is strung with lights and bobs festively on its raft.

But though Noel has a Christmas name, it is tourism that is important to it and all the other tiny Ozark towns. They do well, considering that the biggest attractions are the rivers and scenery. All other businesses—food, beverages, entertainment—have grown up to catch the overflow of canoeists, campers, and picture-takers. Summer sees Route 59 humming with cars, campers, and vans.

The various mayors have a tendency to bemoan the fact that they don't get all the tourists they'd like. But so far, they have not gotten together with anything like a game plan that would enable them to attract more visitors.

"It used to be the roads," says Big Al. "So they fixed the roads, and now they're full of trucks. The trucks are too big, and beat hell out of the roads, and we're back to fixing them again."

On summer nights, canoes glide along the Elk, as if in a black mirror. The lights from the businesses on the shore shimmer in the lapping water. Pale metal canoes and boats slip through the old bridge's arches like teardrops from giant eyes, bearing their loads of lovers.

After many years in the Ozarks, I'm convinced the weather follows no pattern. It's possible to have a sodden spring and a devastating three-month drought the same year. June nights are often as cold as nights in December. Winds come when they please and stay as long as they like—whether it's March or November. As a final touch, local weather forecasters for the four-state area are about as accurate as molasses-filled thermometers.

My first year here—1974—we had a spring as wet as this one. On Dad's property, back in a grove of trees spiking the flanks of a deep gully, a silvery waterfall leaped to life and flowed for some weeks after the rains ceased. The water from it was pure and sweet, in contrast to the sulphury taste of my well's water. (Sulphur water is common all over McDonald County, even in the towns, where it must be filtered. I just drink it. You get used to it—and who knows? They once sold the stuff as a cure-all and youth elixir. Maybe it works. I need every edge, since I can't afford health insurance.)

Springs that flow after heavy rains are called "wet-weather springs." They contribute much beauty to the Ozarks, especially in the dogwood days from late April to mid-May. Bright springs and white blossoms gladden many hillsides that are barely green from budding.

Al and I are about the same age, stuck on the half-century spindle, and we feel an occasional rheumatic twinge when the rain hangs around longer than usual. But more than that is the continual grayness, like a Marine Corps blanket, that drapes each day.

A customer comes in. "Six pack of Mickey's, Al."

"I thought you told me you was on the wagon?"

"Wagon's bogged down in the mud," says the customer. "You think it'll ever stop rainin'?"

"Dunno, but I'm about to start buildin' me a boat."

Outside the rain comes down like silver wires, straight and bright, a loom holding together heaven and earth.

Far below our petty gripes, the water will nourish sleeping seeds, and one day the soil will be as green as a new dollar. And during the dog days of August, when pastures are parched yellow slabs, we will wish for the rain to return—and complain when it doesn't.

※ ※ ※

I must've been about ten when I ate in my first restaurant. This was real uptown stuff for a clod-kicker, and it also marked my first livestock sale.

The sale barn was connected to a lot of high board fences filled with every manner of livestock you could think of, but mostly cattle. A café was on the premises.

My dad and my Uncle Tom often met at the Lawton, Oklahoma, sale barn, although they came from different directions, with Tom living in Cache and Dad near Duncan. Another uncle, Bid, worked in the slaughterhouse at Duncan, where sometimes they let school kids go through on tours.

These tours were *educational,* what I mean—none of this namby-pamby stuff you have today where teachers herd the kids through as if they're on chain gangs. Mostly, our teachers hoped we'd get caught in the machinery or eaten by the animals. They were flexible and democratic.

The highlight of the slaughterhouse tour was where the guy who used a sledge to kill the steers or hogs offered to drink a pint jar full of steaming blood. Right from the jugular, because part of his job was also to bleed the critters the minute they were felled by the hammer.

Now, nothing is dearer to a ten-year-old farm kid's heart than to stand goggle-eyed while something revolting happens in front of him. The girls, of course, quickly vanished, holding their hands in front of their mouths. Well, what could you expect? It just proved they were the weaker sex, as all of us boys knew anyhow. Girls were girls—cooks, housewives, mothers, stuff like that. Boys were critters that could watch a pole-axer drink a jar full of blood.

Anyway, Uncle Tom brought two of his boys, Jimmy and Johnny, to the sale. We were close to the same age, and always glad to see how much trouble we could get into without getting licked for it. The morning passed quickly with a satisfying round of rasslin', chunking rocks at other boys, and risking death by sneaking into the bullpens.

But lunchtime brought me a jolt. I had gone on ahead, curious to see what the on-grounds café looked like. It was filled with cowboys, farmers, and a variety of kids, and smelled deliciously of mingled food aromas. At a long, smoking grill stood the cook, all in white, dishing up everything from hamburgers to apple pie and cheese.

The astonishing thing was, the cook was a *man!*

I scooted back out and relayed the news to Jimmy and Johnny. They called me a liar, flat-out. But with both our dads standing by and talking to ranchers, I didn't dare swing at them. So I said, "OK, smart alecks, you come and see."

They went in with me. Both came out shaking their heads. It was a hard thing to accept, this male cook, because they'd never seen any man get near a kitchen before. Women cooked, and that was that.

"All I can figger," Johnny said gravely, "is he's one o' them sissies we keep hearin' about."

"Well, I cain't figger it a-tall," Jimmy muttered. We were all further nonplussed when Dad and Uncle Tom went into the café and sat down—not ten feet from the guy with the spatula.

"They don't seem surprised, now do they?" I asked Jimmy.

He shook his head. "I reckon they done come here enough t'where it don't bother 'em none."

"It shore bothers *me*," said Johnny. "A *man cook*. I swan."

Later, as we were driving home, I asked Dad what he thought about the cook in the auction-yard café.

"Purty good cook," Dad said. "I had the hot roast beef. How'd you like that pie a la mode?"

"Fine," I said. "But didn't you see nothin' *funny* about that cook?"

"Well, he hadn't shaved in a while."

"He was a *man,* dang it."

"O' course," Dad said. "Women don't shave."

"Would you let a man cook fer you at *home?*" I pressed on, and Dad gave me an impatient look.

"O' course not," he snorted. "I got yer maw t'do that. Why'd I need a *man,* fer god's sake? I swear, your notions just get crazier and crazier the older you get. Ain't no woman gonna let a man come in an' take her job, you oughta know that!"

❋ ❋ ❋

There they stood, scrubbed faces shining, wearing smiles like honeydew slices. Despite the chill of the spring day, they wore short, light skirts—and their purplish knees were evidence that they should have been wearing warmer clothes.

"Hi, Chilly!" they sang out in unison. "We done come t'plant you some flowers!"

My two little visitors were holding clumps of fresh dirt that enfolded what looked like bulbs. (I would learn later that they had gone to the ditch banks, where yellow jonquils grow in profusion each spring, and dug up whole plants—which they now clutched in their muddy little hands.)

"Renae and DeAnn Shaver!" I semi-scolded. "Come inside outta this wind before you catch your death of cold!"

In they scuttled, first laying the muddy plants on the deck, and took seats at the kitchen table.

"What you need is some hot cocoa," I said sternly. "And then you'd better high-tail it home and come back when it's warmer."

As I poured hot water over marshmallows and Swiss Miss, DeAnn, the eldest, said, "Oh, we ain't cold, Chilly, honest we ain't. Why . . . why we even got our coats if'n we wanta put 'em on, ain't we Renae?" (I knew she exaggerated the coats.)

"Shore do," Renae piped.

I set the cocoa down, said "Blow it to cool it," and went to the phone to call their mother, Lucy Shaver.

"Oh, she knows we're here, Chilly, honest she does! We done told her we was comin' an' all. We done planted some o' these yella flowers for her, honest we did."

Her little face looked so earnest, yet underlaid with a forlornness that bespoke such disappointment if she were to be sent home, that I replaced the phone.

"OK," I said gruffly. "But I'm giving you both some denim shirts to wear—it's too cold out there for spring dresses."

"Oh, but it's such a pretty day!" Renae chimed, blowing on her cocoa and then sipping it. She wore a chocolate mustache.

Kids. They rule us from the cradle to the grave, but it is such sweet bondage. Oh, there are kids I don't like, or more correctly whose parents I don't like for allowing them to be the way they are.

In my year as a juvenile officer, I saw what bad parents can do to kids. It's got no better in twenty years, and more than once I've felt that psychological tests and licensing should be the case before people were allowed to be parents. We need licenses to own a car. But to own a child all we have to do is make one.

I watched my two little flower girls, solemnly sipping cocoa, casting an occasional eye my way as if still not sure I wouldn't shoo them home. Both had amber hair, sweet faces, and the shrill piping voices I never could resist. It's hard to be the local grump (a pose carefully cultivated so I can get some work done) under such circumstances.

"These flowers you're about to plant," I growled. "How do I know they're not poison ivy?"

They giggled. Then DeAnn said, "Oh, how silly! Poison ivy doesn't have bulbs. And, besides, we dug these up ourselves, right outta the ditch bank."

The cocoa was about gone, and color had returned to their wind-nipped cheeks. How old were they now? It embarrassed me that I did not know. Each day the Shaver kids passed my gate on the way to the bus stop by the church. There had been many such days, and I had watched all the little Shavers grow from infant, 3, 5, and 7 to . . . ah, now I knew . . . 9, 11, 13, and 15. They had grown up before my eyes.

They lived back in the woods about a quarter of a mile, in a big old house hidden by trees. The Shavers were good neighbors, hill folks to the core, dependable, quiet, minding their own business. But no one would ever accuse them of being rich. The father, and now his eldest son, worked hard at any job offered for every dime.

"Thanks, Chilly," DeAnn said, and Renae echoed, "Uh-huh, thanks," as they trudged toward the door.

"Whoa!" I said, handing them each a shirt, which they dutifully put on. I rolled up the sleeves for them. "Got any tools?"

"Oh, we just use our hands," said DeAnn, holding up the muddy, chapped members. I took two surplus army spoons from a work drawer.

"Just bring these back when you're through," I said, and ushered them out.

An hour later, I emerged from my shed. The shirts and spoons lay on the ground, which the kids appeared to have ruffled some but had by no means dug up. The cold must've got to them. I smiled. The girls meant well, but whatever they'd "planted" hadn't a prayer of surviving this haphazard cultivation.

A year later, on a spring day in 1984, I stood on my deck looking down at the old blue bathtub that sits next to the wire fence surrounding my yard. A row of flowers bobbed in the wind, like golden-headed children.

E ven as a kid, I was a deep thinker. "I wonder how deep that fishin' hole is?" I would ask myself, and myself would assure me it was most likely deep enough for future examination.

However, my mind did run in deeper channels, and some of them liked to have drowned me. There are questions, I discovered, that no grown-up wants any kid to ask.

Take the time I was hoeing corn with Mom. I was about eleven, and there was a brisk wind blowing the red Oklahoma dust into my eyes. The corn was already burnt beyond repair, and I was no fan of hoeing, no matter what muscles it builds. The wind was the final straw, and I suddenly threw down my hoe and yelled, "Dang this danged wind!"

Now, "dang" was pretty heavy duty—as heavy as I was supposed to use, although, like every other kid my age, I already knew all the words my folks tried to keep me from knowing.

"Don't you say that!" Mom scolded. "That's God's wind, and he can do whatever he wants with it!"

This, of course, set me to thinking about religion, and heaven, and that other word, and why God saw fit to blow red dirt in the eyes of little kids. I chopped on for awhile and then asked, "Mom, what do you reckon God looks like?"

Mom dropped her hoe. Then after a moment, she looked at me in exasperation and said, "How in the world would I know? Besides, you don't need to go askin' questions like that."

Now, nothing is as fascinating to children as something they're not supposed to do. When we headed home, our hoes over our shoulders, I was already wondering who I could put the question to again. Dad, of course, would never do.

As luck would have it, I was "farmed out" for a week of helping my Uncle Tom. One night, with my head buried in the silky flank of a cow and with streams of milk singing against the sides of the bucket, I said, "Uncle Tom, what does God look like?"

The sounds of milk hitting his bucket stopped. He peered around the business end of my cow and said, "What makes you ask a damn-fool question like that, Billy?"

"I heard that God made us in his image," I said.

"That's the answer, then. He looks like a human, I reckon." He thought a minute, then added, "'Course, he'd prob'ly be a lot bigger."

"If he looks like us humans, then he can be colored, too—right?"

"*Colored?*" Uncle Tom yelped, for in the 1940s South, that was a possibility that never came up. "No, he ain't colored!"

"But why not?" I asked. "If he made us in his image, and some of us have colored images, how do we know if . . ."

"Maybe we ain't s'posed to know!" my uncle snapped. "Now, let's get this milkin' done!"

If curiosity was the devil's monkey wrench, then he had a whole toolbox in me. Frustrated, I figured that the only way I would get the truth would be to go to the likeliest source—a preacher. We lived far from any church, so I hadn't seen very many. But as it so happened, my aunt frequently had her pastor over for Sunday dinner.

Kids were seen, not heard, in those days. But when the preacher finally finished the chicken and stepped outside into the sun, I was ready for him.

"Sir," I said, "my mama and uncle cain't tell me what God looks like. Just that he looks like us humans but he ain't colored, so . . ."

"*Colored?*" The preacher's face grew a trifle red. "My stars and body, boy, who have you been talkin' to?"

"I ain't been talkin'," I said. "I just been askin'."

"Colored," the preacher muttered, shaking his head as he stomped back in the house. "Somebody needs t'give you a talkin' to, an' that's a fact."

I walked on to the barn, wondering why he was upset.

❀ ❀ ❀

Spring splashed into the Ozarks this year, and at times it seemed as though the only place with more water was the Atlantic Ocean, or whichever ocean is the biggest.

Oh, the sunshine has finally shown up—just in time to keep our skins from mildewing. But for most of this spring, if it was not raining or drizzling, the wind hit you in the face like a wet washcloth the moment you stepped outside.

I happen to like rain, at least more than most folks, and know from past experience that when July and August turn their griddles on, we'll cry for rain while we fry in pain. But that's in the future, and every year we can ignore what lies ahead. It is the human foible we all have the most of.

When it's a rainy spring in the Ozarks, we catch it from two directions, heaven and earth. The saturated soil washes our feet while the sky washes our heads. Missouri's rocky earth is like a sieve, and when the underground water table reaches its limits, runoff is the order of the day.

Then comes the time of the wet-weather springs. Like liquid flowers, water starts blossoming from cracks and crevices, running down hillsides, filling gullies, rushing through long-dry stream beds on a headlong rush to creek, lake, river, and finally the Gulf of Mexico.

Some few of these springs will last almost through summer, especially if there are supporting rains later on. But most vanish within a few days after the rains stop. While they trill and sing through rock walls and tree roots, they cause almost unbearable happiness in the person who stops, tunes out the world, and just watches and listens. Nothing can sing like a new-made spring.

Water is more than a miracle. It brings life more than it brings destruction. And the Ozarks are blessed with good water. For how long? Well, don't ask the carefree souls whose main mission in life seems to be sowing riverbeds with layers of beverage cans.

A few days ago, coming back from another high-priced grocery-buying tour, fuming at a system that underpays farmers and over-charges consumers, my sour mutterings were interrupted by a sound. It was brisk, high-pitched music, catching my ear even above the sound of my pickup's motor. I had taken a beautiful backroad route, down through the vanished town of Coy (where the old, rot-ting grocery sign still clings to the hollow front and walls of what was once a country store).

Down in the bottom, a sparkling creek fattened by spring runoffs chewed at a low-water bridge that looked as if it couldn't hold a goat cart. I rattled safely across and round a bend arched over by giant sycamores and hemmed in by steep hillsides.

It was the hillside on my left that featured the tiny symphony. A virgin spring had burst through the layered limestone and gravel, having nibbled away underground for untold centuries before break-ing loose.

It was a no-nonsense waterfall. Obviously, it saw itself as Niagara and pushed rudely at rocks and dead limbs in its path. Here was food for the soul, in case I have one. I parked, put my blinkers on, and watched nature sculpturing.

The bluff was about 145 feet high on a forty-five-degree slant, stitched with winter-gray brush and trees. Two huge slabs of lime-stone lay on each side of a small cliff from which the stream had emerged. A landslide had birthed them and opened a pathway for the water. (Hearkening back to my days as a college fireman—I was the one who always ground the gears—I estimated that as much water poured from this wet-weather spring as would rush through a dozen hoses.)

On an oak limb high above, a squirrel frisked and chattered. Squir-rels like change no better than humans. This was just one more thing to cope with in a neighborhood that was going to the dogs. Especially since local hound owners had built a kennel near his favorite tree.

But a visiting bluejay could have cared less. He skipped perkily from twig to rock to brook's edge, gave a cautious beady-eyed peek for possible cats, dipped his beak, drank, then flew away.

Even though people live in Coy and the surrounding Patterson Creek area, this tiny glade is secluded—a natural church with preaching by squirrels and jays, who are rarely as dull as their human counterparts. The crest above is sometimes called Tick Ridge, a redundancy since every ridge in the Ozarks, in season, is full of these pesky critters. Well, even paradise had snakes. A little tick-picking is a small price to pay for such grandeur.

It has always amazed me that so few Ozark visitors are willing to take to the back roads and get lost. Yet that is, for me, the true charm of these ancient hills. If you are truly lost, drive in one direction for a few miles and you're bound to encounter someone. (I'm not saying that Ozark visitors inexperienced in the outdoors should get lost while *walking!* Some areas, especially in the Ozark National Forest of Arkansas, are wild and desolate indeed—and hold bones of hapless hikers that will never be found.)

I got out of my pickup, walked to the road's edge, knelt—and brought handfuls of clear, sweet water to my lips. Soon these very hillsides will be fraught with dogwood blossoms. And shortly afterwards, this hollow will bake under a suffocating blanket of leaves.

But for now, this is Eden.

✿ ✿ ✿

L et's go down to Wild Horse Creek an' catch us some fish," Jimmy, a fourteen-year-old neighbor, said mysteriously. He'd shown up at our place early one Sunday evening, just as dusk was bluing the hollows, and was acting mighty odd as he cradled a heavy box. What was in it, he wouldn't say, merely telling me to wait and see.

Also fourteen years old at the time, I liked things about Jimmy other than his being a faithful friend—particularly his ability to squirt saliva directly from his salivary glands. I could spit pretty well through a gap in my teeth, but I'd seen Jimmy drown cockroaches at eight feet, and I'd never known anyone who could make that tiny *squitz*-ing sound as a sliver of spit sped toward its target. It was wonderfully disgusting, and all the eighth-grade girls gave us a wide berth. This was a trait worth its weight in gold, since there wasn't a girl in a thousand who knew how to fish, and Jimmy's squitzing meant we wouldn't have to teach any.

"What's got me riled," Jimmy said, as we clattered through dry cornstalks toward the creek, "is noodlers. It's gettin' so you cain't ketch any big fish—they've all been noodled out. It ain't no more legal than moonshine, and there ain't an ounce of sportin' blood in a whole creekful of noodlers!"

He patted the box, adding, "But I got me somethin' here that's gonna turn things around. And I won't even have t'wet my feet."

When Jimmy sermonized like this, it was best not to interrupt since he wouldn't hear you anyway. There were two kinds of noodling practiced during my Midwest childhood—one using an encircling seine and bare hands and another with a breakable stick attached to a hook and line. The hook was snagged into a fish, the stick snapped off, and then the line was used to bring the fish up.

Hand-catching was much more sporting, of course. The men made a party out of it, feeling in the mud with their bare toes for flatheads or channel cats. When they located one, they'd let out a whoop and dive under to grapple with it. A neighbor once got hold of a real monster and, in the half-hour battle that followed, was nearly drowned. The fish, my dad said, was "in the neighborhood of fifty pounds."

Now, noodling is illegal in most places—not that legality seems to stop poachers. But hand-noodling without hooks was legal when I was a boy, perhaps because there were too few game wardens for enforcement. Today, with a government worker on every brick, it's a different story.

"Noodlin'," Jimmy went on, squitzing a silver arc from his salivary glands, "is the dumbest way t'fish I know of."

"Seems t'me you bragged about going with your dad and doing some once," I pointed out.

"Yeah," Jimmy retorted, puffing now from carrying the heavy box, "but all I got to do was hold one end of the seine while the grownups did all the diving."

We were at creekside now, and even through the thick growths of tall trees and bramble bushes we could see the silver coin of the moon gliding through scattered clouds. Wild Horse Creek was as crooked as a blackjack limb and thick with head-high brush. There could have been a bear fifty feet away, and we wouldn't have known it. It had been a good year for rain, and the hole was brim full of tawny-colored water—and of crappie, catfish, and perch washed in by the floods.

It was a warm, Indian summer night, very still except for a slight scratching in a pecan tree—maybe a coon.

"There!" Jimmy grunted, setting the box on the trunk of a fallen tree whose roots filled the creek like a white octopus. "Now," he said as he opened the box, "I'll show you how to ketch fish."

"Why, that ain't nothing but a telephone," I laughed as he took it out. "What you planning on, Jimmy, talking the fish to death?"

"Hold these wires a second," Jimmy commanded, ignoring my jibe. "I gotta check something and I don't want 'em trailing in the water and getting all wet."

Partly because he caught me off guard, but mostly because I was stupid about such things (we'd never had telephones in our ram-shackle rural houses), I laid hold of the wires. Jimmy gave the crank a rousing twist—and both my elbows took off for parts unknown.

"Ow!" I yelled, dropping the wires. "Dang you, Jimmy, that hurt!" I rubbed my elbows briskly. "I think you paralyzed my arms."

"Right," Jimmy smiled, pleased with the experiment. "Which is what it'll do t'them fish. I'll just feed them wires down into this fishin' hole, and when they're a few feet down, crank the handle. See this big ole round battery, like a thermos jug? That's what shoots the juice. It'll knock them fish silly, and when they float up to the top we'll grab what we want fer a fish fry and skedaddle." Never having heard of anything like this, I resolved to stick around and watch it work.

"Here goes," said Jimmy. The old phone was braced against the fallen tree, its wires disappearing into the water. "Get ready to grab more fish than you ever seen in your life!"

Spitting on his hands, he grabbed the crank and started spinning it like a man cranking a Model T. For several seconds the only sound was the whine of whirling magnets. Then two things happened. Stunned fish began rising from the depths, and a series of excited shouts mixed with splashes erupted from around the bend.

Seconds later Jimmy and I were tearing up the bank, gouged by brambles and ignoring the pain, as three naked men with fire in their eyes crashed through the curtain of brush.

The quiet scratching we'd heard earlier hadn't been a coon at all, but noodlers. And water, as they found out, was a fine conductor.

🦂 🦂 🦂

I n a corner of my three Ozark acres stands an old cedar tree—or what's left of one. It was thirty feet tall until lightning blasted its top off. But it's still alive and green, holding its one remaining limb aloft like some aging one-armed veteran.

The cedar tree is surrounded by black-walnut trees (October's rich harvest) where possum-grape vines twist among the limbs like snakes. On crisp fall mornings I pull off a cluster of the little purple orbs and take a bite of my long-ago childhood.

Growing up in the Depression taught me a lot about eating from nature's supermarket. Possum grapes made good jelly and fair-to-middlin' wine. Wild persimmons brought their unique flavor to cookies, cakes, and puddings. Fresh from a simmon tree, they were the possum's favorite fruit, as an old ditty shows: "Possum up a sim-mon tree, / Rabbit on the ground, / Rabbit say, 'You sonofagun, / Throw them simmons down!'" Many's the time I've hummed that tune during canning time.

My folks were migrant cotton-pickers in season and red-dirt share-croppers the rest of the year. Often there was no crop to share, and much of what we ate came from the woods and creeks around us. But I'll always be grateful for my spartan childhood. I can dine like a lord while others who have never been exposed to native foods must en-dure their growling stomachs.

Most Americans will never know the utter deliciousness of squirrel with dumplings, baked possum, barbecued coon, and Southern-fried snapping turtle (my first taste of fried turtle came from an old black man my family called "The Turtler" because he caught so many snappers and soft-shells to feed his large family). These were the mainstays of many a sharecropper's diet and are still prized today by Ozarkians over fifty.

Besides squirrels, rabbits, woodchucks, and other fauna, the woods were full of edible mushrooms, puffballs, and morels—an edible fungus of the genus *Morchella* so tasty that Ozarkians finding a patch won't tell their own mothers where it is.

Another treat found along creek banks was Poor Man's Asparagus—pale young shoots of "poke salad," a sort of wild spinach delicious with scrambled eggs. We also ate the boiled leaves, but never the horseradishlike root, which is toxic. Pokeberries' purple dye is still used in wine, candies, paper, and cloth.

Eating natural foods takes some learning and getting used to (the finest expert I know in this line—he traps furs and eats all the animals he catches—grew up on the streets of Los Angeles). But turtle meat is crisp, succulent, tastier than chicken, and has a flavor all its own. But baked coon can be compared to delicious sweet veal, while roast haunch of bear (bears were known in the Ozarks until 1957) tastes like roast beef, but is drier.

Preparation and cooking are important, however, since coons and chucks have musk glands and turtles have galls—all of which can ruin the meat if the skinner is careless. Possums are greasy if not properly prepared, and beavers must have their potent castor glands removed.

By the way, the first beaver stew I ever made was called "delicious" by friends who didn't know it wasn't beef stew. Beaver jerky is hard to tell from the beef product. Washed down with good, hot sassafras-root tea, it'll make you a believer in living off the fat of the land.

❧ ❧ ❧

Back when the world and I were younger, so was the automotive biz. So quickly do we adapt to new gadgets, devices, sensors, and stuff, we tend to forget that yesterday's technology was once state of the art itself.

When I hop in my Chevy pickup for a tour around my Ozarks cow pasture, the power steering—long since taken for granted—makes steering far less apt to fracture a wristbone if I hit a stump. I remember reading somewhere that power steering was first tried on heavy trucks and some cars in the early 1930s, but all I know is that it wasn't on the dilapidated pickup that I learned to drive in. Neither were lots of other things—like power brakes and sealed-beam headlights. Radio? Forget it. You couldn't have heard it above the roar and clatter of the engine anyhow.

But let us not be unkind. It was an *old* pickup. It had been "around the horn" twice—and around our bull's horns at least once. As sharecroppers, we invested in a new car just as often as the average panhandler passes out money. The rare times we did change cars, we bought a "like-new used" one—a phrase that always confused me. If it was used, how could it be like new?

Anyhow, on a bright Oklahoma morning in 1947, at the age of fourteen, I learned to drive—sort of. Oh, I hadn't meant to, and my old man sure didn't want me to, but I learned nevertheless.

Our ancient pickup had a battery, but it belonged in a funeral home. That meant getting out the crank—a long Z-shaped tool with two small "teeth" in the leading end that engaged similar slots in the front-end of the crankshaft. (Cranks still came with cars until World War II, but if you find one now, buy it, for it is an antique.)

The engineers will tell you a crank is used to convert reciprocal motion into rotary motion. I will tell you that if the car you're cranking backfires, it will break your arm. Dad always did the cranking— and the huffing, puffing, and cussing. My task was to sit, all grown-up-like, behind the huge black rubber steering wheel and "giv'er the gas" when the motor first fired. Heck, I would think proudly, I'm practically driving this thing.

Dad would give a mighty heave and spin to the crank. Weeza-weeza-weeza would go the engine and then catch with a roar, as I rammed my foot against the accelerator. But one time as I did so I somehow kicked the floor-shift. It engaged with a grinding RRRR, and the old truck and my Dad leaped at the same time—one forward, the other sideways to keep from being run over.

There followed a mighty scene of terror and excitement. The truck was stuck in second, a frequent feat it was proud to be able to do, and the "foot feed" was stuck about halfway down. Dad wasn't stuck. He threw the crank down and came racing after me, shouting instructions. I gripped the steering wheel with hands of iron, eyes glued to the rushing red wall of the barn dead ahead of me. Dead, I thought, I'm gonna die!

"Turn, turn!" Dad cried. "Turn that damn wheel!" I cranked hard, the pickup slewed left—and took off for the rail fence bordering the barn. But I had the hang of it now. Hey, this was fun! Screwing the steering wheel so far right that the old truck heeled over, I ripped right through the two huge opened doors of the barn! Stanchions with astonished cows peering through them flashed past. A stray cat, safe in his barn home till now, scaled a wall as though levitating.

So far so good. The engine howled, the vehicle clattered, Dad once more leapt for his life as I turned the wrong way. But I hadn't hit anything yet, at least.

"Hit the brakes, hit the brakes!" Dad bellowed—at least that's what he told me later. With the engine noise in my ears and the adrenaline in my blood, I couldn't really hear him.

"What did you say?" I hollered, turning the wheel in the nick of time to avoid a mass poultry slaughter. Mom's Rhode Island reds, domineckers and buff orphingtons took to the skies—or tried desperately to, even though they were too fat to fly. The orchard was next. The trees had not been planted with pickups in mind. The narrow avenues, despite my superb steering, soon had apples, pears, and peaches spraying from them as though hit by a tornado. The steaming vehicle finally plowed to a stop in loose earth, lacking power in second gear to pull through. It banged, shuddered, and died. My first driving lesson had ended.

Dad traded the old pickup off for a "like-new used" one the very next day. And made me pick up every apple or pear I'd knocked down, bushels of 'em. I'd pulled through my jam okay—now Mom was into hers. But there was another plus.

I was pretty sure I'd invented the first mechanical fruit picker.

❄❄❄

It is frustrating to be close to a great attraction but unable to market it properly.

One evening, as I listened to the careful tuning of about a thousand frogs, I reflected that if I had just half as many public-relations people as the St. Louis Symphony, I could make the Mc-Donald County Frog Symphony world famous, too.

You haven't heard of the McDonald County Frog Symphony? Well, have you heard of the Celebrated Jumping Frog of Calaveras

County, which Mark Twain reported on some years ago? We are a natural offshoot of that.

But we're the victims of envy. That's my explanation, and I stick to it. The folks who are keen to keep Mark Twain's frog report alive don't want any competition.

There is no legitimate excuse for keeping McDonald County frogs off the national scene. In the matter of symphonic excellence, they have no match. Let me give you a sampling of a program our frogs put on after a recent rain.

First came the spring peepers, tiny grating fifes whose music carried through the velvet dusk for fully half a mile. Acoustics? Why, these boys never heard of such. They need no artificial aids, as human symphonies do. (These little frogs are small, and that is a necessary safety margin. If they were as big as their voices, they could crush houses.)

Another big difference between frog music and the symphony is that the frogs require much less time to tune up. Now, I know that music lovers everywhere will leap to their feet and cry, "But half of the tuning up is just for show!" I don't care. In my opinion, the frogs carry it.

Spurred by the spring peepers, the cricket frogs start clicking. Without a conductor—*without a conductor!*—they establish and maintain a marvelous rhythm. Cricket frogs put a lot of energy into every performance—and I have known oboe players who could learn from them.

Now the medley is reinforced by chorus frogs—their actual name and job description. Finally, with majestic reluctance, the mighty bull frogs come in like runaway tubas.

It's the signal for an explosion of decibels like nothing you've heard, so fiercely bright and tympanic the night seems to sparkle with sound. It is frog symphony at its finest.

You may say what you please, but the McDonald County Frog Symphony can strut its stuff just as ably as the St. Louis Symphony, and no PR is necessary to whet the public's appetite, either.

And just because we are rustics, do not imagine that we are ignorant of dress codes. All our frogs wear tuxedos. They wear them year-round, and each one is form-fitting. What's more, they're not all the same.

I'd like to see an urban symphony top that.

✣ ✣ ✣

There was a lovely rain tonight. Soft, gentle; it reminded me of the tears of the first girl I ever made love to.

And of course, seeing her weep made my own eyes burn, which I hid as quickly as possible. Fifteen-year-olds weren't supposed to cry.

The year was 1948, and I can see her still, a tall, somewhat gawky farm girl with coal-black hair. Skinny to some, she was perfection to me—even though she was taller by half a foot. No doubt we made a funny pair to others in the one-room country school we went to. But a lot we cared. We were meant for each other, and that was all there was to it.

It seems to me as I look back that she had no bust. Well, that's hardly important in the grand scheme of things. Her eyes were the startling blue of wolfsbane—and why no other boy went after her, or what she saw in the class runt, I never, ever knew.

I met her for the first time in the ramshackle farmhouse where we then lived, trying to raise enough cotton on the land to eke out a living. Her parents came to visit mine, and while they talked in the living room, we sat at the dining room table and studied all its scratches. Finally she murmured, "I seen you at school."

"I seen you, too," I said. There was a queer tightness in my chest, but something told me I'd better speak now, or the moment would be lost forever. In agonies of shyness, we looked at each other. Lord, she had beautiful eyes.

"You got the bluest eyes I ever did see," I said, and blushed.

"You got blue eyes, too."

"Not like yores. Mine's too light t'suit me. I shore like yores, though."

She smiled and lowered her gaze. "I like yores, too, Billy."

Billy! She had actually called me by my name. My chest, which was roughly as big as a cantaloupe, swelled to watermelon size—or so I would've sworn. With a boldness I never knew I had, I let my fingers creep towards hers. I touched her hand. *She did not remove it.* Surely paradise itself could not be so sweet!

For days after that first meeting and touching, we wanted nothing more than to be alone. To find some secluded place where we could be Eve and Adam, marveling in our newfound feelings. Finally, one Sunday after she got home from visiting kin, we saw our chance and took it. I led her to a soft, grassy bank under an oak-planked country bridge. It was late in the day. There would be no traffic.

Almost unable to breathe, I croaked, "You ever make love?"

"*No!*" She sounded so horrified, I almost fainted. But I quickly strove to reassure her.

"You seen the movies," I said. "They're always talkin' about makin' love. Well, heck, I betcha *we* could, too!"

"I dunno," she said, her face a beautiful shade of crimson. "I only seen Robert Taylor make love to Eleanor Parker oncet. I ain't sure I really could, Billy . . ."

"You *want* to?"

Her eyes were wet and bright, the deep blue made almost purple by the bridge's shadows. "Yes."

"So do I," I said. Leaning forward, I took her chin in my hand and pressed my mouth onto hers. Her lips did not move, nor did mine. Perhaps a picture would have shown two pairs of lips pressed together like biscuit dough. We didn't care. The planks of the bridge could have fallen on us, one by one, and we would not have moved.

After a long time, she sighed and moved away. We sat apart for a few minutes, in complete awe at what we had discovered. Finally, she whispered, "Well, we done it, Billy."

"Yes, we done it. We made love. Did you like it?"

She daubed at her eyes and said softly, "Yes."

"I liked it too."

So saying, we rose from our creek-bank Eden and headed homeward, holding hands until we were almost in view of our folks.

Boy. What they wouldn't do if they knew we had just made love down by the bridge.

❁ ❁ ❁

Although I was born on the Ozarks' western edge, I left at a young age and returned at an old one. So I had to re-learn "Ozarkian." You won't find books on Ozarkian in any library, but even so that's the official language of the Ozark Mountains of Arkansas, Missouri, and part of Oklahoma.

I've always had a good ear, so I wasn't too worried about being able to pick up the Ozark flavor in the speech of any citizen around Anderson, the tiny town I live in down in southwestern Missouri. (By the way, that's Missourah.) I say flavor even though others would quickly say "Ozark accent." Folks in the Ozarks don't have accents. Other folks from other places have accents. Ozark speech has flavor. (Incidentally, it's a good idea to say "fly-ver"—as in "vuhnayluh flyver.")

Besides relearning the vowels (*Uhee, Ay, Ah, Owuh, Yeeoo*), there are certain correct procedures in abbreviation that those who wish to learn Ozarkian must follow. For instance, right away you should learn *ever* because it plays a large role in the language (try pronouncing that "lain-gwayj"). An example would be, "Ever damn day, m'neighbor's cows are in my garden!" Or: "Ever day it's the same old thing!"

For training your ear, say them about as follows: "Ayuhver dayum dayuh, muh nayuhber's cayohs owr in mah gawr-dun!" and "Ayuhver dayuh ee-ut's the sah-eem oh-wull thang!" *Thang* is a very good word to begin on—it is practically a passport. If you can say *thang* with authority, Ozarkians might not embrace you, but they will let you pass—while they try to figure out where you are from.

Ozarkians are invariably Southerners, or so consider themselves. It is hoped that they will conclude that your *thang* is Southern in origin. If they decide it's not, they might just cut off your air with a rope around your neck—pronounced "yore nake."

Now, my course of study by mail contains several lessons in Speed Ozark. Speed Ozark, as its name suggests, is a fast way to learn spoken Ozarkian. There is no written Ozarkian, because Ozarkians don't write. They use a newfangled device called a *taylafahown*. ("Tay-la-fah-own," but with "own" having an "ow" as in "pow.") In the hollers, of course, they just holler for each other.

Speed Ozark concentrates on special words that convey the Ozark experience. Some of these words are *mule, coon, moonshine, chewing tobacco,* and *chew.* By training your ear and saying, "meeule," "cuhoon," "muhoonshan," "choonabakka," and "chaw," you can pass for Ozarkian—although you had better just try it in the dark. That's so it will make it hard for them to shoot you.

As often as possible, let Ozarkians do the talking. Sometimes this results in three-day silences, but if you use a little corn likker you might have better luck. By letting them talk, you find out about such things as the "non-existent G."

Real Ozarkians waste no time on G . . . unless, of course, they still plow with mules. If they do, you'll hear them say things like "Gee!" or "Haw!"—which tells the mule to go left or right. So if you are an entertainer and learning Ozarkian, bear in mind that if you're telling an audience a joke and hear some Ozarkian holler "Haw," chances are he just has his mule with him.

Naturally, words ending in G sound different—but vive la différence! It brings you ever closer to being understandable in Ozarkian. This is good, because Ozarkians are very clannish. If you obviously speak something besides Ozarkian, they won't accept you for a hundred years.

But if you can master Ozarkian, they will warmly embrace you in about a century. (In my home town of Anderson, a funeral was recently held—an aged gentleman who had come to Anderson from Minnesota forty-three years ago. A local citizen was heard to say, "I hear the new fella in town passed away.")

Now, some G practice: "Are you findin' this lesson hard? You ain't th' cryin' kind I hope? What was that blindin' flash o' light? Oh lord, they're a-shootin' at me!"

Such exercises will help train both tongue and ear, and soon you'll be a-speakin' Ozarkian quite fluently. Also remember to speak *slowww-wly* (three days between utterances is too slow though), and to aid in the deception, have a jaw bulging with a "chaw" and do a lot of talkin' about huntin', fishin', and trappin'.

When you have learned enough Ozarkian to go out in the field, make sure it is a field that does not have NO TRESPASSING signs. Folks in the Ozarks stick very strongly to the Constitution, and are especially fond of the Second Amendment. They keep, and bear, arms with real enthusiasm—and if you are caught on their property, your command of Ozarkian had better be good and your command of hollerin' better be *better* than good.

Hollerin'—and I apologize for not explaining this sooner—has been practiced as a form of communication in the Ozarks for centuries. The word *holler* (meaning a low place between mountains) came about because early-day settlers of the Ozarks used to holler a lot—at each other, at wives or husbands, and at neighbors.

They did some hog hollerin' too, and there was generally hollerin'—along with some cussin'—if somebody set his gun butt down on his toes, got bit by a mad coon, or fell over one of his hounds.

That is why there are *hollers* in the Ozarks, and it adds insult to injury when Missouri mapmakers call these *hollows*. The word *hollow* refers to any receptacle capable of holding moonshine for drinking, and it is pronounced "holla."

"Han' me that holla gourd, wouldje? It's tahm t'do a little drankin'!" But be careful. Drankin' is Lesson Two.

🌿 🌿 🌿

———————————————————————————————————————

I t was one of those bright yellow days that herald spring in southwestern Oklahoma, with new grass neon green and the planting not yet begun. I took advantage of the day to hie me creekward with a pole, some fat grubs, a whiskey-cork bobber, and a hook that could have anchored an ocean liner.

Well, perhaps I exaggerate. But it was big enough to hold the monster catfish that ruled the muddy pool on Big Beaver Creek, where I spent every free hour.

Not that there were many. My family sharecropped when we weren't traveling the migrant trail, and when there was no crop we did whatever we could find to survive. There was no welfare then—not for rural dwellers, anyway.

Naturally, we were too poor to afford a newfangled gadget like a television set. I didn't even know what one was, but would soon find out—in a fishy sort of way.

When I first heard the word, I thought the kid who told me was saying, "Tell a vision." Being acquainted with backwoods preachers who not only saw visions but told about them in "tongues," I was mighty curious.

"Yes, sir," my informant said, "Ol' Junior Fisher's dad done bought a *television* set."

"Oh, corn," I said, using the current slang term for disbelief. "Ain't nothin' can tell a vision 'cept a preacher."

"Boy, are you dumb, Billy Dee," he said. "It ain't nothin' magic like preachers. It's a reddio that gives off pitchers."

The year was 1949 and I was fifteen, albeit with a body and mind of ten, which hampered me somewhat. I went on towards the creek, trying to figure out how a radio could give off pictures.

Finally, I shrugged it off as another benefit of World War II, like prosthetics and the atomic bomb. But in my impoverished rural area, folks were too poor to buy such radios. Except for Junior Fisher, the son of the only rich farmer around here. They had two tractors and a 1949 Hudson Hornet shaped like a bathtub. Their house was huge.

Junior's real name was Clive Jr., but in the way of the South, he would probably be called "Junior" for the rest of his life. A chunky, obnoxious kid, his bragging ways won him no friends—and now he had the first television set in the area. Boy! What I wouldn't give for a look at it!

All this time, in the manner of fishermen, I was fishing and thinking simultaneously. My method was simple: Immerse the baited hook in the brown water, and yank it when the bobber went under.

But fishing palled. The more I thought about Junior's new toy, the more I longed to see it. He was the very devil to get anything out of, especially since I'd bested him in "hoss tradin'" several times—once doing him out of a fine pocketknife.

I was grinning at the memory when there came a tremendous tug on my line. I looked down to see the whiskey cork streaking through the water like a tiny periscope. Then it disappeared, my pole bent double—and the battle was on.

I misgauged the first leap and landed up to my armpits in freezing early April water. "C-c-c-orn!" I yelled through chattering teeth, as my overalls filled—but the fish had urgent business elsewhere, so it was follow or lose him. Sloshing over roots and through mud, I landed the critter ten minutes later—a fine, glistening catfish with a head as big as a platter. Easily the biggest fish I'd ever caught, he would weigh at least ten pounds. Jubilantly, I strung him on my forked twig and headed homeward. The way led near Junior Fisher's house, so I went by, holding the fish behind me.

Hoke, Junior's dad, was a good fisherman, and Junior longed to be like him. But fish followed the example of humans and didn't like Junior either. He couldn't have caught a fish in a tub with a net.

As I passed his house, I stopped, staring at the skinniest telephone pole I'd ever seen. Only it was made of aluminum. Junior emerged from a side door and sneered, "Betcha never saw nothin' like that, huh?"

"What?" I said. "Electricity? Shoot, we lived in a place with electricity over by Lawton, once. It didn't have such a dumb pole, though."

"Billy Dee, you ain't got a brain. That's a antenny for our TV set!"

Casually, I swung the huge catfish from behind my shoulder. Junior's eyes bugged out. "Holy Joe!" he exclaimed, "I ain't never seen no catfish that big! Where'd you ketch it?"

I smiled innocently. "Why, I thought you caught it, Junior, with this ol' pole here, down on Big Beaver Creek?"

His eyes glistened, and I knew I had him. Now I would play him for all he was worth. First, of course, was a look at his television set. Then he had a nifty little .22 that he couldn't hit a mountain with, plus an almost-new baseball glove (he couldn't catch, either).

To make a fish story short, I finagled the dickens out of Junior Fisher that day. I doubt he cared—he'd already put the huge fish in the horse trough, to show his daddy when he came home.

I saw my first television—an early test pattern—and on looking back, recall that it was as interesting as anything today. The screen was small and the pictures tiny, but it was truly an amazing radio.

Was it worth it? You have to be kidding. I'll probably never catch a catfish that big again.

❧ ❧ ❧

When the Roll of Beautiful Things is called on Judgment Day, one item will outshine all others: hominy grits. It comes from corn, looks like sand, and tastes divine.

Long before farming became agribusiness, our family fueled up for a hard day in the fields by eating steaming bowls of grits topped with chunks of homemade butter. As far as I'm concerned, that's the only way to eat grits—although it's OK to substitute store-bought butter if you don't have your own cow. In any case, grits was a food that stuck to our ribs like a cockleburr to a horse's tail.

I have heard that some untutored souls eat grits with sugar and cream. Having mentioned that blasphemy, I'll say no more. Such people would probably be the kind to put sugar in tea to sweeten it and then add lemon juice to make it sour.

Grits is more than just food. Grits is a treasure they ought to have known about in Xanadu. Served with coppery slabs of sugar-cured ham and fried eggs, with red-eye gravy adding its own ruby luster, grits is a dish fit for Kubla Khan.

But most important, grits *is*. A Southerner would no more say "Grits are good" than he would say "Them cream of wheat are bland." Grits is, and shall always be, a singular food.

Grits is also Southern—with the result that you will find the dish on local café menus in the southern Ozarks more than in the northern fringes. Of the 140 million pounds of grits sold annually in the United States, two-thirds are bought down in Dixie. (But the Yankees get their licks in, too. New York and Chicago are the biggest grits markets outside the South.)

Theories abound as to why grits is a rebel repast. One says it's because Southerners were mostly poor and grits was mostly cheap. Another claims that Dixieites were among the first to use Indian foods. Indians, for instance, invented hominy by dehulling corn between stones and treating it to a lye bath. It is from hominy that grits is made. The Indians called hominy *tachahummin,* which in Algonquian means "grinding corn."

The worst period of my life came when I enlisted in Oklahoma and was sent to Arizona for training. They'd never heard of grits in Arizona. Talk about culture shock. Great was my jubilation when they sent me on to Gunter Air Force Base in Alabama, where (Oh, bliss!) a day without grits was as rare as someone singing "Yankee Doodle."

When Southerners leave their homes, it's a fact that they miss grits first and their mothers second.

A search of ancient histories reveals few encomiums about grits, not that this humble food cares about glory. Its duty is to serve and be served—it asks no more. Grits is not the stuff of which poems are made or songs composed. But the dish is loved by the famous and infamous alike.

One of the few accolades came from G. W. Featherstonehaugh, an Englishman touring Dixie in 1837. "Breakfast was excellent," he wrote in his notebook. "Admirable coffee with rich cream, and that capital Southern dish, snow-white hominy grits." (The FDA calls one of America's oldest manufactured foods a cereal, but I'm damned if I will. I don't like the FDA anyway and am willing to bet there isn't a bureaucrat there who has ever eaten grits—as a cereal or correctly.)

The Quaker Oats Company has been making grits since 1879 and is still the biggest manufacturer today. Alas, this once venerable company has fallen upon corporate mentalities—and is producing all manner of Instant Grits, Quick Grits, and grits of just about any flavor except licorice. This is sacrilege pure and simple.

There are undoubtedly people who would shun grits but willingly eat cornflakes. Surprise. Cornflakes are made from grits, according to a spokesman from Kellogg's—which has made cornflakes since 1906. Each of its grits silos holds twelve boxcar loads of the white stuff. The largest size of grits is used for cornflakes, the next size goes to commercial beer brewers, and the smallest size winds up in kitchens and country cafés.

No matter where I travel in the Ozarks, at breakfast time I start looking for a restaurant that serves grits. They can be yellow or they can be white. Just as long as they're genuine hominy grits.

Grits and I go back to my childhood, when the dish was food for both body and soul to my migrant-worker family. Add turnip greens and catfish, you had soul food. Toss a rabbit or squirrel bagged in the yellow dusk of evening into the grits pot, and you had food for the body. It stayed with you like a Harry Truman cussing.

Grits. Can anything so mirror the Southern character? Grits and fried chicken. Grits and gravy. Grits and grits. I've eaten the dish all my life, and never once have I tired of it. I'm writing this at four in the morning, and my one fear is that anticipation of grits to come will make the ending jerky.

I hope the Almighty's wisdom extends to serving grits in heaven, in case I ever have to go there.

If he does, there will be a lot of nectar and ambrosia left over.

🌾 🌾 🌾

I saw one of these fancy new pickups on a city street not long ago, shining like a lightning flash. It was chromed and polished to a fare-thee-well and was so pretty it hurt my eyes. Then on a hunch, I looked in the truck's bed. Sure enough, no hogs.

Pickups are popular these days as vehicles of leisure and owners take great pride in making them more car than truck. But when I was young and energetic enough to spend hours shining chrome, there was precious little chrome to shine. In fact, our farm pickups were trucks of all work and far more substance than shine.

I'm not putting down the new pickups. Times change. But in rural America, they change more slowly than in most places. It's nothing to see, tootling along an Ozarks highway, a clatter-de-bang pickup heading for the sale barn. And in back, grunting and squealing, will be a load of hogs for market.

My late Uncle Hamp was a hog raiser for many years in Missouri. His favorite truck was a rusty, banged-up Chevy that looked like it had been made about the time of the Boer War and may have been in it. No two fenders matched, the steering wheel had whole hunks of black rubber missing, the tires were as bald as a puppy's belly, and the engine produced sounds of fierce combat when first started in the morning.

But, regardless of the outward condition of his truck, Uncle Hamp ran a modern operation, which threw me some when I first saw it. For awhile, I thought I was in a psychological testing lab. Fat, sassy pigs grunted and whuffed as they took feed by rooting against a metal plate and drank by pressing a water button with their snouts.

The climate-controlled individual pig houses were wonders of imagination, kind of Hog Hiltons. But I grew up when pigs—perhaps unfairly—were *pigs*. The italics are mine, because on today's hog farms you mustn't be too free with such nouns. *Pig* generally becomes *hog* among smaller farmers, while big companies raising thousands of animals prefer *swine*.

Recently I saw a television segment about a man who lived with two pigs. The pigs were pets, and the TV crew milked the situation for all it was worth. Why heck, I had an uncle named Bid and an aunt named Sam who raised an orphaned Chester white and turned it into a watch-pig. It was housebroken and took a proprietary interest in the place. On one occasion, after it was full grown, it came barreling out of the bedroom and chased a life insurance salesman clear off the premises. Aunt Sam was always proud of that.

"Ol' Grunter heard that feller a-pesterin' me," she said, "an' told him in no uncertain terms that we didn't want no life insurance. It don't insure life, anyway, an' they oughta call it death insurance instead."

Now, Uncle Hamp discovered a talented hog quite by accident when it broke out of a pen and he hit it with his pickup. The pig, still small, was only skinned a bit and Hamp took him into the house to take better care of it. The pig, a red and bristly Duroc-Jersey with a face like Quasimodo, thrived and was promptly spoiled. It took to following Uncle Hamp everywhere. And one day when he opened his truck's door, the pig scampered in. He hopped up on the right-hand seat, put his hooves on the window-edge and stuck his snout out the window.

From the first time he did it, that was how Squealer rode—with his head poking out of the window and his ear flapping in the wind. Uncle Hamp was always hauling pigs to market, and I used to wonder what Squealer thought, hearing his brothers oinking in back. Probably, "Hey, you suckers—look where I am and look where *you* are!"

In town, after unloading his cargo, Uncle Hamp usually went into the Stockmen's Cafe for breakfast, or if it was *that* time, for what he called dinner, which city folks called lunch. His pet hog just sat on the seat, his head barely visible above the window-edge, waiting and sometimes sticking his head up to view the passing parade.

Once he did that when a teenaged girl walked up to the truck and glanced inside. Squealer rose up with an indignant *oink* and scared that poor girl half to death. I can just hear her telling her girlfriends all about it.

"I just saw me a kid that was uglier'n a *hog!*" she probably said. "Don' go near Hamp Childress's pickup—any kid that looks that awful prob'ly *bites!*"

Hog raising was primitive when I was a boy. Our pigs had running water when it rained and air conditioning when the wind blew. But when it comes to quality of life, there ain't a pig in any of those fancy houses that wouldn't rather be out rooting for acorns in the oak woods.

✿ ✿ ✿

Like buttermilk spilled on a hillside, daisies whiten the east pasture. The largest patch is almost an acre in size—a fact that doesn't impress my dad.

"They take up pastures," he says. "Cows won't eat 'em, so what good are they?"

To the farmer, daisies are weeds. In large numbers they often must be taken out because they affect the economics of making a living. But because Dad's small herd is only to supplement his Social Security, he has so far not brush-hogged the creamy patches that add such festivity to the grasslands.

From now through summer there will be flowers—and flowering weeds—of many different kinds scattered throughout the Ozarks. Often I bemoan my lack of botanical knowledge, for I don't know the correct names of 95 percent of the flowers I see.

One of my treasures is a 1934 *Webster's New International,* found at the Indian Creek Trading Post in Anderson and still in good shape. In it, a fine color plate depicts fifty American wildflowers—a wonder lacking in the 1979 version I have.

Some of the names are nicely poetic: butterfly weed, checkerbloom, jewelweed, baby blue-eyes, dutchman's britches, prairie smoke, meadow lily (the one we call tiger lily)—and dozens of others. The old plates are glossy and beautiful even after all these years, a tribute to the time when bookmaking was an art and not a disaster.

This year also promises a huge crop of blackberries, for never have I seen such an explosion of blossoms. Mounds of green bushes burst with blooms like some Fourth of July Vesuvius Fountain. Already little green berries are forming, tiny embryos covered with prickly hairs—the better to discourage birds and other berry-gobblers.

Blackberries make wonderful jam, and the best I've ever tasted was given to me by Eileen Finn of Hazelwood, Missouri, via her husband, Ralph. I made the mistake of leaving it where my son could find it, though, and no bear could have performed a more thorough robbery.

I do some robbing myself, picking selected wildflowers for a table vase when there are masses of them. They won't last as long as domestic flowers, but they have a special beauty all their own. (No one should pick from roadsides or from posted land, however.)

Something comes over me in daisy fields, and I take off running like a colt. Yes, it is the height of silliness for a middle-aged man to go galloping through acres of white daisies, but it's better than pushing them up.

Dad's house is a riot of spring colors, too. The red lava of roses spills from vines by the driveway, and flowering azalea shrubs border his white plank fence with their pink and white blossoms. Tan house, yellow mailbox, red iron wheels flanking the drive—and red hinges and latches on the outbuildings.

The chicken yard, polka-dotted with hens, will soon be hidden by morning glory vines threading the chicken wire. And in the rich manure of the corral, pink thistles will grow as tall as a man only to be trampled down by livestock at loading time.

I never tire of the infinite variety of wildflowers and weeds, of pastures mellowed by the low, rich sun, of jade-colored grass covered with dew like diamonds in a rare tiara. If I were religious, I'd have a name for it.

The ever changing tapestry of God.

🌺 🌺 🌺

Winters are cold on the Oklahoma plains, with a cold that burns like a branding iron. Blue northers howl out of the hills, whipping the yellow prairie grass that is fit only for hardy range cattle and as cover for rabbits and wildfowl.

It was there one winter that my father gave me the Christmas present I've never forgotten.

Dad loved to hunt, but as a sharecropper he had little time. Still, he never missed a chance to take his dilapidated old shotgun out for cottontails or quail. Made about 1890, the single-shot 20-gauge had a pitted barrel and a loose hammer, and for such a small gun it kicked like a prairie mule.

Dad had wanted a new shotgun for a long time, but there was never enough left over when the year's dues were paid. He had his eye on a Sears bolt-action .410.

"A .410 is plenty good for the huntin' I do," he would tell Mom, as he flipped the catalog pages.

We sharecropped two half-sections that lay wide apart. That winter, Dad trustingly agreed to let a rancher run some cows on one of them for a few dollars. But nothing was said about numbers, and the rancher flooded the land with cows—rangy horned Herefords that stripped the grass like a plague of locusts. All Dad could do was pocket the meager check and swallow his anger, knowing the cows would go when the grass was all gone.

One night Mom and Dad sat talking at the kitchen table, the kerosene lamp casting an amber glow on their faces. The Sears catalog was open, and I heard Dad say, "We had a pretty good year, and I'd sure like to get this here shotgun."

Two weeks later the postman's Model A slewed through the mud of recent rains. Its horn went "oooogah!" and Dad went out, signed something and returned with a grin as big as a kid's at Christmas. He was lugging a long, skinny parcel. Even Mom was smiling as his excited fingers ripped away the cardboard to reveal a shining .410.

"Hot dang," he said, his eyes sparkling, "Ain't she a dilly? What do you think of her, Son?"

"She's a dilly, all right," I said admiringly. Dad let me have the first heft, but after that a crowbar couldn't have pried him loose. He rubbed the .410 with one cloth, shined it with another, oiled the action, worked the action, wiped the action dry, fired the action, and whipped the gun up and down as though following bobwhites on the rise.

Loading and shell-ejecting came next. He fingered the red shells with their yellow brass caps as if they were pearls of great price. To us they were, costing about a nickel apiece when a nickel went as far as a dollar does now.

"Well," he sighed finally, "everything checks out. In the morning, we'll go try it on some rabbits."

The sun glittered from a thick armor of frost, so that pastures seemed diamond-clad as far as the eye could see. We donned our mackinaws against the cold December wind and headed out. Dad's coat was blue, mine red with yellow grids, so the sun bounced brightest off me. In the distance we saw cowboys chasing steers, the herd parting like a cordovan sea to let them through, mud flying from their hooves.

Dad's first shot was at a fleeing cottontail. The rabbit kept on scooting, and Dad looked chagrined. "I'm damned," he muttered. "I *sure* thought I had him."

"Let me try," I said, but he managed not to hear me.

"I *did* have him," he insisted, staring at the shotgun.

I asked him again.

"I ain't sure you're big enough to handle this just yet," he replied—his way of saying he didn't want to let go of his new toy. I was disappointed, but I understood. It was the first new gun he'd had in his life. Before long, I'd be glad he held onto it.

The cowboys' shouts cut the cold as they roped or chased cows, as much for sport and to stay warm as to check the animals for disease. But the steers didn't like it. The minute they were released, the angry beasts charged their tormentors, who laughed and yippeed as they spurred out of danger. These range cattle were lean and quick, with horns like oversized railroad spikes.

"That's crazy," Dad snorted, steering us around the herd with a comfortable margin. "The damned fools are running weight off them cows and making them mad as hell to boot."

We angled across the pasture, boggy now as the winter sun took hold and the frost melted. The cowboys sat on their horses and watched with tight grins as the sharecropper and his ragtag kid walked past, out for rabbits to fill a skimpy pot. No love was lost between the horsemen, who fancied themselves rodeo stars, and the men who farmed what had once been open tracts of rangeland, although for the most part they tolerated each other pretty well.

A cowboy broke from the group, spurring after a steer, rope spinning around his head. The loop landed. The big steer *brawped* and hit the ground. Just then a jackrabbit bolted from a bush and tacked off across the prairie. This time Dad tracked him right, the .410 boomed, and the jack flip-flopped into death.

At the same time, the cowboy was releasing the steer, who was mighty mad. He charged the group, which scattered with wild yells. Then, noticing Dad's sweeping movement and spying my bright mackinaw, he wheeled from the riders and thundered down on us.

I was bending to pick up the rabbit when I saw the steer.

"Run, Bill!" Dad yelled, and Lord knows, I tried. But my legs were paralyzed and felt like lead. I wanted to run more than anything, but I couldn't move. The cowboys saw what was happening and raced after the maddened steer, but I knew they'd never reach him in time. Then, inexplicably, my feet started working. I started running—slipped and fell flat on my face.

Dad was skinny and not very tall, but he moved like lightning between me and the charging steer. The .410 swept up, back, and he stepped into that bull like DiMaggio into an easy pitch. There was a sharp *crack*! and the animal slumped to its knees—as parts of Dad's shotgun sailed in every direction.

Slowly, he gathered up the splintered wood. He stared at the .410's bent barrel as I watched, the dangling rabbit forgotten. The cowboys held back, saying nothing as this sharecropper wiped mud off the broken remains of the only new gun he'd ever had.

Finally, Dad turned and said to me, "Let's go home."

He lost a shotgun that day, a Christmas present to himself. But he gave me the best present a kid could have, one I've been enjoying ever since.

2

Late summer and talk
on a good friend's porch,
talk of why the midwest
is so mid.

Clouds rumble like tanks
on the dark skyline.
The radio warns
of cyclone weather.

The big elm
in the yard loads up
and fires a salvo of birds
at the coming storm;

A momentary hush,
then a fierce edge
opens the tree
like cut flesh

and ozone is thick
in the air. We sit
as though we've been
struck by lightning

until a cool wind
blows from the banked clouds,
bringing rain
and reason back.

When I was fourteen, living on an Oklahoma red-dirt farm whose chief crop was cockleburs, my future was already tucked under the straw mattress I slept on. It consisted entirely of a brochure from the Professional Author's Program (PAP), sponsored by "some of the finest colleges and universities in the land."

I recognized at once that this was my ticket to a glorious and glamorous future. I could speak English. I could also spell it. What more did one need to become a writer? I salivated over PAP's promises, realizing as I read the brochure that I was that rarity—a "born writer."

The brochure challenged me with wonderful things like similes as exercises. A simile is a kind of comparison of objects that are not alike. These were usually set off (the brochure said) by *like* or *as*. However, the phrase "like similes as" in the beginning of this paragraph is not a simile. I don't know what it is. It works, and that's all I care about.

The brochure wanted to know if I could complete such phrases as "Red as a . . . ," "Cheeks like a . . . ," and "Quiet as a . . . ." Unhesitatingly, since I was at an age that made me privy to such knowledge, I scribbled "Cheeks like tan," "Red as a punched nose," and "Quiet as a kid putting clothespins on a sleeping cat's tail." I was particularly proud of this last, because it showed I could master long sentences as well as short ones. With a smile (for I knew I'd won the prize of free tuition), I mailed the answers to PAP and sat back to await fame and fortune.

Soon my test results came back. As I had known they would, they screamed congratulations at me. "You're a born writer!" they shouted, bugled, crowed, implored, and otherwise informed me. "Although you did not quite win the free tuition prize, we are happy to offer you a special discount rate, and. . . ."

I saw what the special rate was, gulped, and became downright glum. Where would a sharecropper's kid get the monumental sum of $78.95?

Well, the heck with it. I would write anyway. But first, I had to decide what I wanted to write. Poetry? Fiction? Westerns? Mysteries?

Science fiction? Inspiration flashed immediately: I would write them all.

This resolved, I sat down, dashed off a western story and several poems, and mailed them to *Jim Hatfield's Western Magazine*. The labor had consumed half a day. Clearly writing was something to be rationed, lest it take all one's time. But these had sprung with such full-blown grace from the brow of my inspiration, I had no doubt I could write part time—say, a novel a week—and still have time for all the glamour and romance of my new profession.

Soon the stuff I'd written came back. The editor urged me to waste no time in seeking another line of work. I knew immediately that he was just testing me—his was bad advice meant to be ignored. I also suspected he was jealous of my talent. Editors, after all, must sit all day in little offices, whereas writers jot down their stuff or dictate it fresh from dreams at night—then take the rest of the day and go fishing. I knew at least the latter was true because I had seen pictures of a famous writer named Hemingway. According to the photographs in newspapers, he was always fishing or hunting. I began to wonder if he owned a typewriter. Another wonderful author named Faulkner rode horses a lot (after foxes, as it turned out)— aristocratic behavior that was unparalleled. No doubt about it. The writer's life was the life for me.

For the next ten years, I wrote steadily, and received numerous notices of my advancement. With some variations, these notices said, "We're sorry, but this isn't what we need at the moment." How warmly encouraging! They were explaining that the situation was momentary.

Years, and postmen, passed. Many more such messages came, gentle reminders that the publishing world was still aware that I was practicing my craft.

One fine April day, fourteen years after I'd first mailed the brochure, I received—ah, miracle!—a rejection slip that was actually signed. It was signed "The Editors" and it was from *Reader's Digest*. I praised the day I had chosen such a rewarding occupation.

I wrote a novel, got married, had children. The novel was about my years as a paratrooper, and one stirring passage went: "The huge C-119's loomed from the dawn like giant footballs, their butter-knife tails limned against the light." I had just discovered *limned* in the dictionary, and wanted to use it while it was still fresh. I would have no clichés or hackneyed phrases in my novel.

My dialogue, too, was good strong stuff: "Awright, you $$$&?@! troopers, gitcher $$$&?@! on that plane! We gotta $?$@@!%¢ jump to make." It was a line uttered by "a burly sergeant named Prentiss." I did not see how the book could fail.

But fail it did. I was still impoverished and unpublished, still pounding the keys, when my long-suffering wife—tired of scrambling eggs over a candle because the electricity had been stopped— divorced me. She was nice about it, explaining that, really, thirteen years was a generous time to devote to art, mine or anyone's. She married a bookkeeper and is sublimely happy.

Before leaving, she handed me a note that said: "I'm sorry, but this isn't what I need at the moment."

Now, so many years after sending off that fateful brochure, I live in a shack, write by kerosene lamplight, and occasionally get so low on food I ask my cats to share a mouse.

I have this vision of me, my life over, standing before the Pearly Gates. St. Peter—ever alert for writers—will saunter over, smile, and hand me a slip of paper that says, "Sorry, but you aren't what we need at the moment."

❧ ❧ ❧

———————————————————————————————

The twisting two-lane highways of the southwestern Missouri Ozarks have claimed their share of victims. Most of them have been young, for teenage motorists and the age-old hills have an affinity for each other that sparks duels.

There is a legacy, too, of roaring Mercuries in high-speed chases during the days of moonshine smuggling and bootlegging. Whatever the cause, it is in the very air—and so it is that, as regularly as the seasons, twisted automobiles are winched up from the bottoms of gullies while their drivers are borne on eerie sirens to hospitals in Gravette, Arkansas, or Joplin, Missouri.

"They never seem to learn," Dad said, after the death of a neighbor's teenage son, "that these mountain roads ain't freeways."

Now, more than half a century after infamous U.S. Highway 71 was cut through these hills, change is coming. The once-gravel highway was paved many years ago, then was rerouted, leaving the old highway to become Missouri Highway 59. Old U.S. 71 passed through the old bath spa of Sulphur Springs, Arkansas, where decaying well-houses and hand pumps that still work are the badges of an era that saw excursion trains from Kansas City and St. Louis "comin' to take the water."

"When they moved Highway 71," a Sulphur Springs woman told me, "they reduced a town of thousands to hundreds in just a few years."

New Highway 71—known not so fondly as Suicide Alley to motorists and truckers—was rerouted through the Arkansas town of Rogers, thus assuring the growth of this now-thriving city. It has tripled in growth since moonshine days and is the retirement home of famed baby doctor Benjamin Spock.

Highway 71, according to popular belief, claims more lives each year than any other Missouri highway—so many that, for a while, motorists with macabre senses of humor sported bumper stickers saying "I Drive Highway 71—Pray For Me."

Now, years after the rest of the interstate system was completed, word is that soon all of Highway 71—the main freight artery into the northwestern Arkansas hills—will be four-lane.

The old U.S. 71—the new Highway 59—twists like an asphalt anaconda from Anderson, Missouri, to beautiful Siloam Springs, Arkansas, some 50 miles distant, and then on 150 miles more to end in the Ozark town of Heavener, Oklahoma.

All along its route are remnants of once-sturdy towns grown old. Highways are life in the Ozarks, as they are everywhere, and Highway 59 is no longer the main artery it once was. The names of the towns along 59 are Indian, French, and Scots-Irish—Gravette, Cherokee City, and Gentry in Arkansas; Watts, Westville, Baron, Piney, Sallisaw, Spiro, Panama, and Poteau in Oklahoma.

Most of the route is mountainous and beautiful, a long lonely drive back into time, into America's yesterdays. But none of it matches, for me, the beauty of the 20-mile stretch of Highway 59 between Anderson, Missouri, and Gravette, Arkansas, via Sulphur Springs.

I have driven this road hundreds of times in my years in Anderson, and each time is as magical as the first time. I love to drive it in the wee hours, when the dark highway is all but deserted except for an occasional lonely trucker roaring through the night, no doubt wondering whether this tree-lined truck route will ever end in civilization. They drive in tense terror much of the time, knowing that dozing even for a moment can catapult them into deep canyons that eat big trucks at the rate of several a year.

But this is a dreamscape for me. I drive when the moon rides high and full, when alabaster light coats the dark Ozark forests like metal filings. At the top of the hill near The Cove, between Lanagan and Ginger Blue, there is a large metal marker that gives the history of McDonald County. Here, I can stop and peer at the highway, at the rare vehicle passing at 3 A.M.

On down the hill, which twists and turns above deep ravines, is Ginger Blue, a resort founded in 1915 and "handed down" through the years from tourist to tourist as one of the quaintest Ozark resorts.

Highway 59 is a rare drive day or night, but for me nothing matches the glowering Noel bluffs deep in shadows, kissed by moonlight, that overhang the highway, or the silver road-posts flashing past like dragons' teeth in my headlights, or the cold glitter of the Elk River that parallels the highway for several miles.

On these trips I seem suspended, something unborn held in a metal womb, feeling the great life force of these timeless hills pulling me toward some kind of reckoning, some kind of destiny, some kind of birth.

❄❄❄

Highways have personalities. The one I was on had a sprightly, no-nonsense one, slapping against my pickup's tires in brisk rhythm every time they crossed a crack. I was headed out on the first leg of a continuing journey around the Ozarks, rounding up stories for the *Post-Dispatch,* and Anderson melted from view in my mirror as I headed north on U.S. Highway 71.

As hills and trees flashed by, white blurs from a rich blossoming of dogwoods, my mind went spinning back to a time when the boy that's still somewhere in this middle-aged body also sat behind a wheel.

In 1959, fresh from the service, I was barbering in a two-chair shop in Richmond, Virginia, where I'd been handed my third honorable discharge (in spite of a court-martial) and $235 in mustering-out pay. I worked six weeks for a crotchety old man, and my biggest take—after his cut—was $16. Even living in a boarding-house (two meals a day) for $35 a week could not be handled on such wages.

But an attractive young teacher lived there, and although I was still in my "Aw, shucks, ma'am," stage and could only admire from afar, I did make so bold as to ask her to read a short story I'd written. Lacking a high school education at twenty-six made me in awe of teachers. Real teachers, surely, would know a lot about real writing.

Alas, not so. She found the piece "compelling and powerful." Two years later, in college, a professional writer found it "random, incoherent, ungrammatical and puerile." He forgave me the "ungrammatical," saying that grammar wasn't always the key log in the writing jam.

But then the writing wasn't in yellow-lined notebooks in lead pencil—it was on the wall. My calories were running out. I had to break away and go where there were jobs. That meant California, 2,631 miles west.

A few days after my discharge, I had lucked into a 1946 Packard sedan. Gleaming black with red cinquefoils on its hub caps, it was a princely car. The old man who owned it had put it up on blocks thirteen years before, when he developed cataracts, and had been much taken with my open-mouthed admiration of the still-glossy vehicle.

"You ain't got much money, have ye, son?" he said, peering at me through his cloudy eyes. I said, no, that I made $16 a week and had only $150 left of my mustering-out pay. He dropped his gaze to the dusty garage floor. Then, slowly, as if telling an old friend farewell, he walked around the Packard, touching it with his hands.

"Gimme a hundred and twenty-five and go," he said huskily. As I backed the silkenly purring sedan past him, I saw him looking at me with the steel-bright gaze of a man who is crying.

I left Richmond as broke as any hobo. Even at four gallons for a buck, gas was high if you were penniless—which I very nearly was. As I rolled the Packard towards Nashville, there was in my mind the thought that maybe I could pick up a buck or two playing guitar in a bar.

But in Nashville, guitarists were a dime a dozen, and all of them were better than me. I aimed the beautiful silver swan on the car's hood towards Oklahoma. I had kinfolks there, if I could get that far.

I made Little Rock—a sprawling dusty town, then, nothing like the metropolis it is today—before my money gave out. I was in the Ozarks now, but scenic appreciation does not sprout from a growling belly. I made job rounds, found none, was all but perishing from hunger. It was March, still cold, which made me unpack the rolled-up Levi jacket I hadn't worn in Richmond—and find in a sidepocket a crumpled dollar bill.

Good old George! I was wealthier than J. Paul Getty would ever be as I slid onto a worn stool in a diner run by a sweating man with a lobster-red face. He ladled red beans, sausage, sauerkraut, and corn-bread on a big oval platter and watched me shovel it in—*after* I'd given him 65 cents.

"Lordy, boy," he said, "yore belly must thank yore th'oat's been cut."

Afterwards, knowing I had no choice, I took my barber tools and went to a local barber college. "Anybody want to buy a good set of tools?" I hollered.

"What you askin'?" said a black-haired, heavy-set kid.

"Hundred bucks. They're worth twice that."

"No dice."

"Sixty."

"Forty."

He knew he had me. I knew he had me, and he knew I knew he had me. I took the money and shucked the dust of Little Rock as fast as my newly gassed chariot could take me.

There were other adventures, perhaps for some other time. The Packard got me to California in style, but I was busted again. I was standing next to my prize possession at the curb outside a bar when a man stopped to admire it.

"Don't suppose you'd part with it?"

With sinking heart, I said, "I gave a hundred twenty-five—can you go that?"

He peeled off bills so fast they were smoking.

❀ ❀ ❀

One by one they drop away, not the old but the young, vanishing into that great sadness—they who ought to have had so many more years to live.

These are young people I knew as children, who came first out of curiosity to see the bearded hermit in the walnut grove. Finally, they came to spend hours, their eyes bright with new questions as fast as I answered the ones they had asked.

I am the richer for having known them; I, a curmudgeon with kids whose smart-aleck ways raise my anger. But there was nothing that was ever rude about the Hitt boys, Matt and Mark. There was a kindness and consideration in them that was far beyond their years.

And now, Matt is gone. There is something unbelievable about it all, the flower-draped casket, the stunned mourners—and outside a sun burning just as bright as if a part of it had not gone out.

None of us ever thinks of the deaths of our children, for the pain of the thought makes it unthinkable. And then one day, or one night, word comes from a sheriff or a hospital that you'll never see your son or daughter alive again. I have three sons. I think about it.

Matt must have been all of twelve when I first saw him—a stalk of a kid with haymow hair, a hangback little stringbean who took a while to get acquainted. And then the questions came. What was a writer? Did I get paid for putting words on paper? Where did I go with my battered camera case and equally battered old Saab— sometimes staying away weeks?

Matt and Mark sat at my table, sharing their dreams of tomorrow, of what they'd do when they were eighteen at last, no longer cubs, and able to forsake the family cave. It is the natural order of things, but there is a sadness to it that's also natural.

Mark grew up, graduated, became a meat cutter and a good one. Matt was restless and grew up the hard way, equal parts of pride and passion. Handsome, tall, he would suffer no insult. He was quick with his fists and over a period of time developed a reputation as one of the tougher McDonald County kids.

From time to time, he and his brother would drop by. Once Matt showed up with a yellow-and-blue eye. There was a glint of something else besides curiosity in his gaze, now. But he was always the soul of respect to me. On one trip, the brothers brought a prize rooster, and I loaded my aging Konica and took a series of color shots. One appeared in a national magazine, and both boys were pleased by that.

Matt, too, passed eighteen, and high school—but his restlessness was still upon him. A best buddy was Shane Walters, the son of a skunk skinner and fur buyer. Early on, I'd met Ivan Walters and his wife, Shirley, and braved the dreaded skunk shed with its hundreds of hanging hides—to the vast amusement of Ivan.

Shane was a good skinner, but he shared Matt's quest for excitement, for "something to do." There was drinking, fighting—and there was some fast driving. Whenever I ran into Mark, now married and with a baby, he shook his head and talked about Matt's fights.

One day Mark told me Matt had run into someone who was not only tougher, but mean. Matt was beaten unmercifully. He lost teeth and was hurt by kicks. It appeared, when he recovered, that he'd had enough growing up the hard way. He eased up, settled in, won a scholarship to a local college and began taking classes.

Both boys were tall young men now, filled out to twice my size. Other bodies hid the skinny kids I'd taught to throw tomahawks and allowed to look through my telephoto lenses. The gears of our lives clattered along as they turned us towards our destinies.

And then one day Shane, his mother, and Matt Hitt took a trip into the South. Near Columbus, Mississippi, the car struck a bridge abutment. Shane's mother and Matt were killed in the accident.

I suppose, in the vast scale of time that has weighed all of man, the death of any one of us is of small significance and soon forgotten. But in photographs and memories, ghosts are as sharp as faces were, and in the recall of past times lies the sanity of us all. We are all part of each other. No matter how we battle, we began from the same glorious seed—and are the less when any petal falls away.

✼ ✼ ✼

O ne night after a heavy rain, I stepped out onto the porch and took a deep breath of the freshest air anyone is ever likely to breathe.

Dad's two dogs, visiting our one, were investigating clumps of Bermuda grass, perhaps in hopes of rousting a field mouse. The sky was still cluttered with clouds, and the moon suddenly sailed out from behind one like a discus flung by some Olympian.

It was almost twelve years to the day since I had fled a broken marriage and an overpopulated state in hopes of finding a quiet place to write and recover. I hadn't really understood the impracticality of the idea. Now, looking back, it amazes me that I was able to make a living, albeit a very sparse one, as a free-lance writer.

I recall that every work week was seven sixteen-hour days long as I wrote dozens of queries, researched dozens of articles, and made dozens of tough, often hungry trips. There were no vacations, and I never was able to afford heath insurance—far less a dental plan. Few editors would give advances, so my meager bank account was always near-empty as I slept in car or pickup beside many a forgotten highway.

I remember one freezing night in my old 1964 Saab, the best car I ever owned (it's still owned by a lady in McDonald County). It was late, I was exhausted, and so I pulled over on a mountain road and tried to sleep.

In the end, the magazine I'd done the story for refused it. I'd just read that the magazine's owner, who paid wretched rates, was spending a week on his yacht. In a fit of anger, I wrote him a letter telling him what I thought of him, his magazine, his editors, and his yacht. I'm sure he read it and got rid of his yacht right away.

There were many such incidents in the decade that followed. But it was all for a good purpose, because it shaped whatever I was for what I would eventually become—a storyteller. There were times, though, when I did not know, myself, why I kept on at such a futile occupation.

Now, I've been in one place—the Ozarks—longer than I was ever at any other, and I don't know why that is, either. Once I starved out and left for greener pastures with a petroleum firm. But when that ended after a year, I was never more glad to return to a place than I was to my three acres, which fortunately, I hadn't sold when I took the job.

Almost any Ozarkian that I talk to is just as puzzled about this curious place and its curious mystique. It gets to you. In time it becomes a panacea.

"Folks leave," said one old-timer, "and folks come back."

"You'll be back, Chilly," a friend said to me when I left—and sure enough, I was. It takes some thirty years, but we return if only to retire far from the madding crowds.

There is a loneliness about the Ozarks at night that I love. It's a feeling of such solitude that putting it into words is impossible. A man can feel like the first man at such times, on the first night after the Creation.

Ozark nights are good for thinking. After a rain, the little tree frogs are sated and silent. Clouds roll across the sky like puffy juggernauts, and the moon plays ping-pong on their tops.

Follow the bouncing ball. Follow the yellow brick road.

Perhaps in the Ozarks, I've found my Land of Oz.

There may be some folks in the Ozarks who are able to give directions that I can understand, but if so, I have not located them. That's not entirely their fault. I've been known to get lost in the bathroom. Even after years in southwestern Missouri, I am frequently amazed by the free-wheeling and original style the natives impart to direction-giving.

Because they have festivals galore down here, and contests within the festivals that cover everything from pie-making to the prettiest man's legs, I'm wondering why they don't have a direction-giving contest. The loser would be turned loose in the Ozarks and asked to find his way out in, say, a year. If required to proceed solely on instructions given him by other Ozarkians, I believe he could count on spending Christmas in the backwoods.

There is the story of a tourist who, thoroughly confused by the twisting, two-lane roads, spotted an old farmer plowing with a team of mules. (This was some years ago.) "Say, there," he hollered, "I'm trying to find the town of Rocky Comfort, and I understand it's somewhere near here."

The farmer whoa-ed his mules, cut off a chunk of Mickey Twist with his pocketknife, and with the wad firmly in place, explained: "Wal, sir, you head on down this road till you see a big old oak tree on your left. Take a right. Half a mile further, you'll see a big ol' barn off to your right. Make a left turn there. Then a quarter of mile on, you'll see a cow in a pasture, an' . . ."

"A cow in a pasture!" exclaimed the motorist. Oh, now wait a minute, this is silly—I can tell you right now that such information is of no use to me!"

The farmer spat, turned back to his mules, and said over his shoulder, "Why didn't you tell me you couldn't read road signs?"

A variation on this theme is that after lengthy and detailed instructions, the traveler says, "And will that get me to Rocky Comfort?" The farmer answers, "No, sir—but you sure will see some mighty purty country!"

Folks down here don't mean to get you lost. Indeed, if guilty of anything, my Ozark neighbors practice overkill when it comes to playing guide. They are truly trying to help, and that means they wish to be as clear as possible. Hence the generous *amount* of directions most Ozarkians will generally give on being asked. I have found, for example, that I can usually count on being given at least three choices of ways to reach my destination.

A friend of mine who owns a gas station is one of the best multiple-direction-givers I know. He is so good, I can't begin to recall the actual directions he once gave me—I will have to imitate them as best I can (using fictitious names).

"Sam, do you know Jim Pickle?"

"Knowed him all my life," Sam said, as he squeegeed the windshield.

"Can you tell me how to reach his place? Ain't it out on 76?"

"Well, you *can* get to it on 76—pull your hoodlatch—but that's only *one* way . . ."

"I'll take the easiest way, Sam," I said hastily.

Visions of getting lost and driving miles and hours out of my way began rising in my mind. Sam studied the oil dipstick, unmindful of my agitation. This was a master misguider at work, and he was going to do it right.

"Well, lemme think . . . yep, you take 76 out past the Skelly station, 'bout a mile, and take a right down through Coy . . ."

He peered at me from under bushy brows. "You know where Coy is?"

"I know where it used to be."

"Still is, just ain't been no store there for a few years." Sam stooped, reflected for a moment, then said, "Well, you could get there that way, but I'm thinkin' maybe you'd do better to not turn off on the Coy road."

"Why not?"

"Might get lost."

"That's why I'm asking you for directions, Sam, so I won't get lost."

"Well, I don't give no *guarantees,* y'understand." Sam looked at me quizzically until I nodded, then continued. "OK, so go ahead through Coy if you've a mind to, and take a left at the fork, just over the little bridge that crosses that creek—Patterson, I think it is."

"Patterson is near Coy?"

"Right by it."

"Two towns right together."

"No," Sam said patiently. "Patterson is a *creek.* Anyway, keep left till you pass the dentist's country home. Go on till you see the Mitchell Cemetery, pass it and hang a right on that dirt road . . ."

Pausing, he said reflectively, "On the other hand, the *next* turnoff will get you there, too, but it leads across a low-water bridge that I ain't been across in years. Might be washed out . . .

"Or—I just remembered—you can even reach that ol' boy's place by takin' 76 to 43, then comin' in the *back* way . . ."

"How much do I owe you, Sam?"

"Twenty bucks for gas, nothin' for the directions."

They were both worth the price. I got lost almost immediately, and finally wound up in Seneca, where I called Jim Pickle and told him I'd be a bit late—and how could I find his place, anyhow?

✻ ✻ ✻

When my first marriage ended in California in 1974, I took it hard. It was bad enough that it wasn't even called divorce anymore. Now it was called "dissolving a marriage." "They're going to dissolve me," I remarked to a vague barroom acquaintance. He turned out to have been dissolved for years. What's more, he vowed never to get married again. Chances are, he's wrong.

After finally admitting that my wife, who had filed for the divorce, had more courage than I did, I said good-bye to the thirteen years we'd spent together and pointed my second-hand car towards the Ozarks. I had been born along their southwestern edge, and Dad now owned a farm in Missouri.

Like an aging bear licking its wounds, I hibernated in a house trailer surrounded by walnut trees. I must have seemed a strange man to my rural neighbors—bearded, a writer, and, worse still, from California.

The Ozarks were still sparsely inhabited and that suited me fine. It was several months before I ceased being a hermit, and during that time I had many tormenting thoughts about my three young sons. The court had wisely decreed that they remain with their mother, soon to be remarried, rather than gypsying around with a journalist. I could visit them at any time, of course, and they were free to spend summers with me in the Ozarks.

When my wife's remarriage took place (to a solid, reliable man with a nine-to-five job), I came out of my trees and took stock of things. I was just one speck in the cosmos, and no matter how seriously I took myself, four billion other humans neither knew nor cared if I existed. If I was going to be a star, it would have to be in my own galaxy. I set about planning the kids' first summer with me and getting my emotional house in order. Editors were assigning me work again, and the morning sun no longer looked weary and dull.

Given an assignment that took me back west, I swung by San Francisco and picked up my boys. The trip back to the Ozarks was wild: I spent much time reaffirming my fatherly rights. The Order of the Palm was bestowed often and did at least temporary good. Somewhere in Utah, the boys got so rambunctious I stopped the car and made them do laps in a roadside park until their unbelievable energy was depleted. Back in the car, they fell peacefully asleep, and I got some driving done.

When we reached the farm, the boys piled out with whoops of glee. After visiting with their grandparents, they raced out across the pastures and into the woods. It dawned on me, as I watched their exuberance, that children of divorce don't always have to be the social victims movies once made them out to be.

A couple of decades ago, children of divorced parents were the subject of great concern to sociologists and psychologists—who saw in them the criminals and alienated citizens of tomorrow. The concern still exists, but now at least it's known that if divorced parents do their best to go on being parents to their children, the end result can be much happier. In fact, research has shown that a marriage that holds together "just for the kids' sake" is likely to do more harm than good.

In the woods, my oldest son managed to find the only poisonous reptile within miles. He raced back to inform me of his treasure.

"It's a copperhead!" he said excitedly. "He's lying under an old log!"

"Don't be silly," I said. "I've been living here almost a year, and I haven't seen a copperhead yet."

But I reckoned without my son's Little Golden Book on reptiles. When I pried myself from the typewriter and went with him, I saw that it was indeed a copperhead—beady black eyes and all. When I moved the log I angered the snake, and he struck at the toe of my boot. The fangs didn't penetrate, but the venom he squirted turned the leather momentarily dark. With a yell, I grabbed my son and leaped back. He was delighted with my reaction.

"It *is* a copperhead, huh Dad? A *real* one!"

I captured the snake with a forked limb, and today my oldest son still has it, preserved in formaldehyde in a half-gallon Mason jar— probably the only kid in San Francisco to have his own copperhead. The jar is labeled crookedly, "Caught in Missouri, 1975."

When the three boys weren't splashing in the water tank or the creek, they hunted squirmy, croaking, hissing critters of various descriptions. Chris, my oldest, soon added a black snake (later released alive), while six-year-old Jason and four-year-old David Daniel specialized in tree frogs and turtles. David soon became the acknowledged expert on tree frogs, at times directing a whole symphony of the chirring little creatures. He could stick them on his body or make them balance amazingly on a thumb or finger. Meanwhile, Jason was embarked on an absorbing study of how many times a box turtle would climb over a brick barricade he had built.

The summer ended all too quickly. When I took them to the airport, Jason said, "We know you're not coming back to California, but can we come back to the farm again if we're good?"

I looked back on the final sad years of my marriage, remembering my sons' fears and uncertainties as they heard the endless bickering. I was no longer ashamed that my marriage had not lasted a lifetime. My kids were happy, doing well in school, and had the best of two worlds—not to mention two sets of caring parents.

Hugging all of them in the circle of my arms, I said around the lump in my throat, "You bet—but only if you're good."

Their mother says the ploy only works when summer is near.

❈ ❈ ❈

All of us need sympathy from time to time, or at least we believe we do.

But you can't just go charging in when you want sympathy. As in every art, there's a right way and a wrong way. The wrong way will get you an irritated look at best, and at worst a scathing comment. "You've got my sympathy," folks will growl, and walk away.

Or you can try my way. I go after sympathy by approaching likely prospects with a woebegone expression on my face. I generally choose nuns, or—if I can find one who hasn't worked maternity—nurses.

That is, I *used* to do it like that. But now the nuns are mad at the Pope and the nurses are mad at the doctors, so any sympathy they have in reserve is kept for themselves. That makes sense, as they won't get any from the Pope or the doctors. (You have my sympathy, ladies.)

Actually—and I might as well confess it—getting sympathy these days is darned near impossible. (Except from my bosses. I asked them for a raise awhile back, and they said, "You have our sympathy.")

When my electric bill—huge from burning the midnight oil—

came due, I went to the company's office and said, "I can pay you in sympathy." They got a little amused over that one. Two had to be given mouth-to-mouth resuscitation.

Searching for sympathy in the Ozarks can sometimes bring results, however. Even the biggest problems down here are eased by sunsets and good gardens. But solace can take some curious twists, for with so little sympathy around, competition is fierce.

Let me illustrate the point. Not long ago, I received a wound on the upper part of my forearm. It grew red and angry, and only my Spartan courage kept me from making a fool of myself over the pain. I hollered for half an hour, but in the privacy of my three wooded acres. My sole comfort was that I nailed the critter that did it. There is one less mosquito in the world today, I can tell you.

I went into town, a conspicuous bandage on my arm. I'm not the Band-Aid type, believing that when the taxpayers sent me to Army medic's school they meant for me to use my skills.

Dan Townsend, the local newspaper editor, was ambling around and he asked, "Did you break your arm?"

"No," I whimpered. "Does this look like a sling?"

"Well," Dan chuckled, taking advantage of my crippled condition, "you *are* pretty well known for slinging." Then he added, "Knowing you, that's probably no more than a skeeter-bite under there."

I left him, resolving to cancel my subscription to his newspaper—even if it did make a good bug-swatter.

At the venerable First Baptist Church, which is seventy-five years old, I encountered two ladies. We knew each other slightly, and one had read some of my stuff in the local paper. Here, I knew, was sympathy made to order. They were church-goin' folk, they were women, and they did not wildly applaud the feminist movement.

"'Pears you got hurt," one of them observed. She was graying and motherly, bless her. I explained that I did have a rather serious abrasion under my bandage, but that the prognosis wasn't a bad one.

"Well, then, you are a lucky young man," she snapped. "I have got the arthritis so bad I can barely brush my teeth! Also, my gall bladder was taken out a year ago, and now the doctor thinks it has grown back and I must go through all that suffering again! As for genuine agony, sir, I get the gripes in my vitals till I cain't hardly set still! Try *that* sometime if you want to feel pain."

"Mildred's a-tellin' the truth," the other lady said. "But at least she doesn't wake up with catarrh a-chokin' her and her liver a-killin' her. If it wasn't for Doan's Pills, I don't know what I'd do." She lifted her specs up on her nose and peered at me. "What did you say was the nature of your affliction, young man?"

"Oh," I said, "it's nothing. But let me assure you ladies of one thing. You have my sympathy."

There was a loud knock on the back door of my trailer—the door that sports a large sign, "USE OTHER DOOR PLEASE." The other door was the front door. The back door was strictly for fast getaways in case of tornado or fire.

Wondering who stood outside and was unable to read, I opened the door. A wild-eyed man holding a black book stood there and he immediately began shouting at me.

"Thou art fallen, fallen!" he cried. "Thou art become the habitation of devils, and the hold of every foul spirit, and the cage of every unclean bird!"

I admit I was startled, but nobody calls me a dirty bird cage and gets away with it. I escorted the gentleman past my sixteen-foot livestock gate (his frightened wife peered from the window of the ancient car he drove), explained that anybody within miles was more religious than I was, and bade him good day.

I have not had good luck with religion in my life, having had the wits scared out of me as a tot by a backwoods Oklahoma preacher who came at me speaking tongues.

Six years later, when I was nine, Mom frontslid from where she had backslid and was "saved" by a large woman who had "the call."

This lady was notorious among us younger kids because she had a thriving black market going in wire hangers—impossible to buy during World War II's steel-scarce days. She would offer us kids a penny apiece, and we would filch hangers from our parents' closets. She resold the hangers for a nickel.

To a kid on summer vacation, Sunday school is still school, and school is still jail. I had been too recently freed from such restraints to enjoy them anew, but although I can outrun her now, Mom was faster in those days. With my ears smarting and ringing from being reamed by a washrag on a pencil, I was hauled off to an evening service.

The fat lady was already exhorting a handful of women. No men— and no other kids—were in the place. For the life of me, I could not understand her attraction. To me, and to the other kids my age, she was just a fat lady with short hair and a loud voice who had cornered the market in coat hangers. But tonight she was at the top of her form, jiggling and dancing among the rude benches, hurling her pink hands skyward, pausing rhythmically to hear "Hallelujah!" or "Praise be!" from her flock. And then she saw Mom and me.

"Bring forth that darlin' child!" she hollered, and Mom obeyed with such speed my shoulder socket popped. Down went Mom on her knees in the dust. Down went the other ladies, surrounding me in a saintly swarm. The grocery store owner got on top of a bench and bawled, "Lord, make the devils leave this here child!"

Well, I had had enough before even coming in the door, and this capped it. But there was no way to break free from my human corral, or I would've been gone like a rock from a slingshot. To say that I was scared by all this excitement is being too charitable. I was petrified, so that when, after several minutes of screeching, the lady got down on her knees and put both her hands on top of my head, I went a little crazy.

"Waugh!" I squawled, struggling to rise and leave the premises. But all those kindly hands knew right away it was just demons in me, working to get out, and they were firm in their concern. The more I struggled, the tighter they held on.

At last, exhausted, I slumped and began sobbing. It was the right thing to do, because the fat lady got her face down in front of mine and smiled like a crescent moon.

"I knowed we could do it!" she crowed. "This here child is now saved from the demons and devils."

The stars were holes in the heavenly tent as Mom silently led me home, where she went into her room without speaking. Dad was reading a paper by the fire. He glanced up once, but that was all.

Evangelists, lay or ordained, work hard to bring joy and peace to millions. But since that long-ago night, I have admired, revered, and respected another kind of Christian entirely—the quiet Christian who gets strength for this hard life from his religion, is a good citizen, and is content to keep his religion and not generously try to give it to others.

✻✻✻

"Have you ever been lonely? / Have you ever been blue? / Have you ever loved someone / Who didn't love you?" So go the lyrics of one of countless songs about human loneliness.

Another old one, and a favorite of mine, is Andy Williams's "Lonely Street," which I used to hear as I lugged a heavy leather bag along my mail route in Reseda, California, in 1959. It was a huge hit and seemed to pour from every house on every block. "Where's that place called looooonely streeeet?" Williams would wail, and somehow, in some curious way, my own lot in life seemed better.

Humans need grief as much as they need jobs, and songs of loss or heartbreak, or being abandoned or being alone. Such songs are part of the blues, largely the color of life itself. Few pains can equal the agony or heartbreak of a man or woman who, in utter helplessness, goes on loving someone who no longer cares.

Indeed, most songs, when you think about it, are sad songs—whether in rock, folk, or pop genres. A poetry anyone can understand, songs take life's pain and make of it a kind of pleasure. If we do not weep outwardly, certainly we weep inwardly. It is our tribute to a lost paradise, whether real or imagined—a happiness that can never be.

I don't know about you, but I've been lonely a lot. Sometimes I've been lonely even when living with another person—for much of this emotion comes from a wistfulness that does not take reality into account. No matter how I might wish it, there is no perfect woman. No matter how I may idealize it, there is no perfect romance. In such sad truths lie the seeds of loneliness.

When my first marriage took the deep six, I chose a solitary life and for years rarely saw anyone. I went about my work, started and threw out at least ten novels, completed another book of poetry, and wrote hundreds of magazine articles to earn my daily bread. But people played only a tiny part in my life in those days of divorce shock.

We never know until it is over whether a course we've taken is right or wrong. What's done is done. I finally came out of my self-induced hermitage, not because loneliness drove me, but because I needed human contact to be able to write.

Still, there are times when I crave loneliness and need it like a drink of water on a parching day. In its calm silence is a recharging of the spirit, far from the crowd, free from the endless demands of others.

And even after I've left Solitude's Cave to come back out into the unreal world, certain sights or sounds can take me instantly into a profound sense of solitude—of the aloneness of living and dying. Be not afraid of loneliness, some philosopher-poet once said, for it will make you strong.

Things that make me feel lonely, and therefore in touch with my spirit and the spirit of man: A solitary child in a rubber-tire swing; wheat fields of beaten gold that seem to flow forever; a man sitting on his suitcase by the road waiting for a ride; a child trudging up a dusty road; the huge black clouds that precede an Ozark storm.

Yes, being lonely isn't all bad. Sometimes it's one of life's wonders, like the coming back from some faraway place to the here and now of home. There's no better way to know yourself, to make peace with your broken dreams, to celebrate the dreams achieved—to look forward to dreams that may yet come true.

🐾 🐾 🐾

Rabbits are so much a part of rural life that I couldn't understand "Easter bunnies" as a child. Rabbits that laid eggs? Why, any kid who ever walked a furrow knew that *chickens* laid eggs. Why not just have an Easter chicken?

But when I became a father, my three boys had no such hang-ups. California city kids, they accepted without question that a giant invisible rabbit laid colored eggs in grass and bushes on Easter morning. Their philosophy could be couched in six words: "If it's candy, don't ask questions." But one year a decade ago when they visited me on the farm, they found out the hard way that rabbits don't lay eggs.

I saw Chris, Jason, and David—ages ten, eight, and six at the time—infrequently because their mother had remarried. Only if a free-lance trip took me westward was I able to collect them and bring them to the Ozarks for a summer sojurn.

They took to country life like ducks to water. One day, Chris came running in with a tiny rabbit cupped in his hands. He was very excited, and so were his brothers.

"I took it away from a dog!" he exclaimed as I carefully examined the tiny, trembling creature. I didn't relish telling my son that a dog's powerful jaws usually inflict fatal injuries on something this small. But to my surprise, the only damage to the squeaking infant was two puncture wounds in the side of its neck. I disinfected these with peroxide, explaining that even if the rabbit survived its wounds, it might die in captivity.

"That's why it's not a good idea to keep wild animals, Son," I said. "They don't always do well when they're caged up."

"I'll take real good care of it, Dad," Chris said seriously. "It won't die."

And it didn't. He built it a home in a large, open-topped box, and with that unstinting love young children can lavish on pets, nursed the rabbit as if it were the last of its species.

Amazingly, Bunrab—as Chris called him—flourished and grew. My son wanted to know what he ate in the wilds. I replied that rabbits ate seeds, grasses—and, of course, gardens.

"Lettuce!" he cried, and from then on showered Bunrab with all the greenery he could find. He also experimented with various cereals—and the little bunny selected corn flakes as his personal favorite.

Weeks passed, summer waned, Bunrab grew. Soon it would be time to return the boys to California and school. Chris and the rabbit—who was no longer a baby—had grown very close. Bunrab readily came hopping when Chris crackled a corn flake or whistled. One morning, all three boys were hunched around the breakfast table, absorbed in something I couldn't see. Coming closer, I saw Bunrab balanced on his hind legs like a squirrel, crunching away at a flake of corn held daintily between his forepaws.

And then one sun-flecked day, as a cooling breeze swept through the walnut grove, I locked up the trailer and the four of us headed west. I had agreed to let Chris take Bunrab, even though I knew his mother might be less thrilled with his prize than he was.

For the first thousand miles, Bunrab was the ideal traveling companion, kicking up his long hind legs, twitching his nose and—once—making a puddle on Chris's folded-up jacket. Then something transpired to change him. He became restless, a little crazy, racing around in the station wagon, scrunching up under seats—so I exiled him to his cage. He was a muscular, sleek young adult. What drove him to these extremes was undoubtedly hormonal in nature.

"Son," I said soon after we crossed the Utah line, "we're going to have to let Bunrab go."

"Let him go?" Chris's face and voice were both forlorn.

"He wants to find a mate," I said. "He wants to start his own family. Nature is telling him what to do, son, and nature is a very powerful force."

Trying to find a bright side for his brother, David asked, "Will he lay eggs for Easter, like the Easter bunny?"

"Oh, David," said Jason. "I *told* you about that Easter bunny stuff."

David screwed up his six-year-old face and retorted. "Well, I don't believe *anything* you tell me!"

Suppressing a smile, I said, "It's more likely Bunrab will produce a lot of little bunnies. But who knows! Some of them may become Easter bunny helpers."

And so, in a brushy area of Utah, we let Bunrab go. He hopped out of his box, sniffed the strange air, sniffed the ground, nibbled a green grass stalk—and hopped away. Twenty feet into his new life, he stopped, looked back at Chris and then, as if in celebration, leaped high into the air. When he came back to earth, he gave two huge bounds—and vanished into the thicket.

Back in the car, I said softly, "Son, I know you'll miss him. But from his point of view, his new life is a lot better than being cooped up in a box all the time. And remember this—he would never have grown up at all if you hadn't rescued him from that dog."

"I know," said Chris, turning his face towards the fleeting landscape to hide the tears that ran down his cheeks.

❧ ❧ ❧

I cut across the hayfield the other day to check on Dad. The rains had forced us to a late cutting, and though Dad feared much of the crop would be ruined, he lucked out and most of it was saved.

The hayfield is the central acreage on Dad's farm, and until he makes his crop no cows are allowed in it. So the grasses grow so tall they eventually bend like bright, weighted wires, each with its own type of seed—for Dad believes good hayfields, like good herds, consist of mixtures.

I was halfway across the field when I spotted the first buzzard. That's what we call them, although turkey vulture applies equally well. The birds were north of my path, but I stopped to watch them soar—for they do it with such exquisite grace you forget that in them Beauty and the Beast are forever wed.

Like great gray-black gliders they razor the air, tooling each current as though they have some hold on it, some way of making it do their bidding. The tiniest curl of a wing-edge feather and the huge birds seem yanked by strings, feathered marionettes in an aerial ballet.

But it is hard to feel good about buzzards. They stink something horrible, and the reddish pebbled scaly head-folds, with the hooked and powerful beak, do little to lend enchantment. And now there were four of them, swinging in wide circles then hurtling towards the ground. They are not hunters. Something was dead or dying there in the tall yellowing grass north of the hay field.

For the end of whatever it was, a dance of dark angels was taking place above it. Soon, its earthly struggles over, the strange and unknown spark that is life would leave it. The summer heat would take instant toll. Within an hour the dead creature would be "high"—its perfume gliding on the wind as if on wings itself.

I set out at a jog, for it might have been only an injured calf in the grass and weeds, and I could carry it to the barn or go get the truck if it was too heavy. Sometimes calves can be at death's door, but a good vet can save them. (What a far piece they have come since the old, frock-coat-wearing "hoss doctors" of my childhood. I still remember one of them holding a bowl of turpentine to the umbilicus of a horse with colic, supposedly to cure it).

Carefully threading the strands of barbed wire—once so easy when I was a kid thin as a cornstalk—I went to the spot the buzzards had been circling. The huge birds themselves had soared upward, until they were just tiny specks. But their eyes were sharp as needles. They knew what was happening. And in a moment, so did I.

An old dog lay stretched among the yellow stalks, obviously breathing with terrible difficulty. He wasn't very large—about spaniel size—and by anyone's measure, he'd be no more than a mutt.

I saw, then, why he labored to breathe. There was a hole oozing dark red blood from his chest. It could have been made by a bullet, the long fang of another, larger dog, or perhaps even a form of cancer eating through his chest cage. I knelt and stroked his rough old head, but he was too weak to even notice. I wished for my pistol, so I could end his suffering quickly.

How had he come so far—and from where—leaking blood all the way? I'd never know. What held him now, in unbreakable talons, was the great invisible vulture that waits for all of us.

Nature. Life. Two words without feeling. Feelings develop, they aren't born in us. At least I don't think they are. But none of it mattered to an old dog, peering with glazed eyes into a dark, winding tunnel—as dark and winding as the slowly narrowing circles of the buzzards above him.

❊ ❊ ❊

I knew him for many years as a man whose only god was Bacchus. He believed in a magic that deceived, an amber genie who sang to him of wonderful things and splendid dreams—and brought the tawdry and nightmarish instead.

But it wasn't all that bad, he kept telling himself. And over a period of years, he came to believe that he, not the genie, was in control. And having won control over such a power, he called it forth more and more—just to prove he really could control it.

I was with him in the Army when, little more than a boy, he did the manly thing and went drinking with his buddies. Never mind that he was horribly ill afterwards, and that the next morning brought such agonies he wanted to die.

All that passed of course, and so did the years. Years and wives and children, and bar brawls and car wrecks. Once in an Oregon saloon I was with him when he got a little too loud for the lumberjack at a table. The brawny young man was drinking, too, but not as much. The lumberjack told him to shut up. He stood up and hit the lumberjack in the jaw instead. He felt good about that and grinned in triumph. That was when the younger man got up and hit him.

And hit him, and hit him, and hit him.

He said later through swollen, scabbed-over lips that he had "laid some good ones on that bum, too." But the truth was, he was overweight and out of shape—and already in his forties.

Once in a foreign country, he got hold of some bad whiskey. It said scotch on the label, but black marketeers had cut it with small amounts of wood alcohol—a deadly poison. Fortunately, he drank only a shot-glass full. But even that amount built a terrifying fire in his guts and put him in bed for the whole weekend.

I was with him when he saw a buddy boast that he could chug-a-lug two steins full of vodka, and didn't try to stop him. Urged on by drunken, cheering pals the youth guzzled the liquor, dribbling it down his chin and onto his uniform. Halfway through the second stein, his eyes glazed over and he fell forward onto the table. Frightened, the men called for the medics, who came and took the unconscious boy to the company aid station. There, a doctor worked hard to save him, even injecting adrenalin into his heart. But he was dead. The autopsy showed four times the amount of alcohol in his blood necessary to kill him.

Yes, the man I'd known for so many years was there. He saw it all and returned badly shaken to his barracks. But the next night he went out drinking in an effort to forget how his buddy died.

We were in college together after the Army. Both of us were hard up for cash, so he became a connoisseur of inexpensive wines. He would tell classmates who visited his shacky abode, "This Carlo Rossi isn't a bad wine—the secret is to let it breathe for a spell."

Some of the wines he drank could have doubled as paint thinners, but all that counted was that they contained alcohol. Even so, he either didn't have—or more likely didn't admit to having—any serious problems until he was in his middle thirties. True, he'd known alcoholics far younger, including his nineteen-year-old buddy who had died. But that was them and he was him.

Something happened, though, and he became a much worse

drunk than ever before. A frequent bar patron, he got into fights. And once I watched with horror as he sped through a red light at sixty, his eyes locked straight ahead like a zombie's. Thank God it was 2 A.M., and there was no traffic. Still, he was a lucky man.

Many times his patient, suffering wife would have dinner ready, but he would be in the American Legion bar, drinking and refighting his war, staggering home hours later too drunk to eat. He was a teacher and was often hung over in class. He excused this behavior by saying that everyone else drank too.

And then late one terrible night, I came upon him in a bus station latrine, sobbing and vomiting, beating his right fist bloody against the wall. He was out of his head and kept crying, "I don't want my sons to see me, I don't want my sons to see me!" But there were no sons, for he was divorced and they were far away.

Finally, as if some mist had moved in, I lost track of him for quite awhile. How long it was before I saw him again, I honestly can't say. It might have been days. Perhaps it was months. But one day there he was again, in the mirror, looking back at me. And as we stared at each other, he smiled and spoke.

"Congratulations," he said. "I hear you've joined AA."

"We've joined," I retorted, and he chuckled.

"Right you are. Well, we had to do something and we were the only ones who could, you know."

"I know. I just wish we'd done it sooner."

"The past doesn't matter," he said. "the thing is, we did it. And by the way, you'd better hustle. We've got a meeting tonight."

※ ※ ※

On the sunny windshield of Dad's maroon pickup, a drama is being played out. Dad and I are standing, elbows on the hood, talking politics. As I often do, I listen with half an ear while my attention roves elsewhere.

Wedged beneath the wiper blade, a spider lies—dark, furry, built like a tiny tank. Few engines of destruction can match it. Its fangs, venom, and powerful eight-legged body make it more than a match for anything but spider wasps. The largest such wasp has a shimmery blue body, orange wings and has the odd Latin name of *Pepsis*. Its larvae feed off a stung spider until the spider dies, literally eaten alive.

The little deaths of little things are mirrors of ourselves. Yet so cold and calculated is death in the insect world, we'd rather not look. We are above such robot actions. We keep our killing emotional.

Just as we have a balance of power, so does all life—for life feeds on life, and in the process produces death. "Bugs kill other bugs to eat / While we think butchered cow's a treat." I forget who came up with that jingle, but few of us ever think about the gentle herbivores we kill so our dogs and cats can dine.

What's with this spider? Has it already eaten? There are laws that must be observed—nature's own, stern and immutable. And those silly flies—look at them—circling so near its lair while the hairy monster watches and waits. A fly skitters up the glass, turns, flirts its wings in the spider's face. Perhaps it has acted on impulse, or possibly it doesn't know the spider is there.

Now the spider emerges, slowly at first, then moving—almost rolling like a tank on treads—toward the swarms. It's hard not to think of a zebra herd and a stalking lion. The herd acts nervous, almost giddy, as it plays out its role in the coming tragedy. Suddenly the lion bolts from the brush, singles out its prey, and in moments it is over. The zebra lies kicking out its life while the lion holds it by the throat. Even before the first bite is taken, the rest of the herd is back grazing again.

The spider advances, pulls back, spins suddenly. It can't make up its mind. (It sees the flies through jeweled, octadic eyes—eight tiny prisms gleaming in the sun.)

The flies act so strangely. They appear to pay no attention to the spider's approach. Surely they see it. Does some tiny aura surround the killer, lulling its prey into a false sense of security?

The spider advances again. The flies ignore it. They play among themselves, visiting, gossiping, performing courtship dances in the warm sunshine. Occasionally, a couple will meet, hormones will go wild, and mating will begin. Such honeymoons are brief and programmed to happen. The spider slinks nearer, watching, waiting. It knows from experience that breakfast will soon serve itself.

The flies continue cavorting with joy—but now it is a *danse macabre*, being shadowed by death. Another couple meet, sing in delirious joy as they mate. The spider creeps closer.

The flies still seem unaware of the spider's approach. Can it be that they play the odds against dying—as airlines do? Perhaps fly statistics somewhere say, "Risk it, take a chance, only so many are meant to die."

And then, incredulously, it is over. The spider simply walks up, seizes a mating pair—and skitters back to its lair under the wiper blade.

"Hell's bells!" I shout, making Dad jump. "It got both of 'em."

"Both of what?" Dad is puzzled. He had been talking about bumping off Khadafy.

"That spider got both of those flies."

Dad says nothing. I watch as one fly, drained of its vitals, rolls limply down the windshield. The spider starts on the other one, empties it of calories, snugs back under the blade.

Nap time.

🌿 🌿 🌿

Summer takes its toll of feathered young. Perched on the threshhold of freedom, some fail to sail—and plop awkwardly to earth, where, as often as not, a cat or snake lies waiting. So it was with Mister Meadows, which my youngest son took from the declawed paws of Voytek, one of our two tiger-yellow cats.

Mister Meadows was a baby meadowlark, just at that turn in his life when feathers replace hairy down. But he hadn't fallen from a tree. Meadowlarks get their name from building dome-like nests hidden in meadow grass. This juvenile bird with its squawky cry and gaping beak had been unnested by my cat.

"Can I keep him, Dad?" David asked, and although I had misgivings, I said yes, provided the bird wasn't injured. Cats may appear to be just having fun, but their paw-slaps are like karate blows. There was also the possibility that Voytek had bitten the bird and it was wounded.

We took Mister Meadows—for so David had christened him—to the vet, who said he looked OK, and to feed him small rolled balls of canned dogfood. David put him in a small chest, and he took the dogfood bits greedily.

Even so, Mister Meadows lived for only twenty-four hours. We don't know why he died. Perhaps he suffered a fatal wound that we had overlooked. Or maybe he missed his mother, and his nest, and the shock of meeting the world on its own terms was just too much.

We took him out into the patch of woods behind the trailer and buried him. And there in that lonely glade, with the wind working the leaves and the boys standing by, I played a sad requiem on my harmonica for the small life that never got off the ground.

Who among us has not wondered at, or been exasperated by, the shenanigans of birds? They've played a part in my life, especially when I was a boy. I used to dream of having a "talking crow." I've long since come to doubt that splitting a crow's tongue will enable it, with coaching, to talk. I've never seen such a bird in action. But that's what they used to tell us.

"Split a crow's tongue an' it'll talk to you."

"But how do I catch one, Grandpa?"

"Sprinkle a little salt on its tail!"

Mostly, sharecroppers hate crows—for crows are "share croppers" themselves, the lousy thieves. At one time in the 1940s, they got so bad in Oklahoma that a group of farmers set dynamite charges in the trees along a creek where the multitudes had their roosts. Finally, all was ready—and on a given night the sky turned brilliant orange and rained feathers, twigs, and wetness.

A long time later, I wrote a solemn verse about the incident. The opening lines went:

> The day the wheat was ready,
> Dark forms fell like rain.
> From high on their struts of wind
> The whirling raiders came
> To mutilate and shatter
> The bronze ranks of grain.

I can remember skies black with crows for miles, their hoarse caws filling the air as they smudged the sky like dingy passenger pigeons. Scarecrows were useless against them, as was the binding twine that farmers strung on tall poles over their fields. The theory was that the crow, the smartest of all birds, would "distrust" the simple yellow lines as possible traps. More effective were dead crows left dangling on field fences or tall poles.

Today, crows are few and far between, their numbers reduced greatly in the past forty years as we chip slowly away at the earth we live on, replacing its animals with ourselves. Eventually, like lemmings, we may breed ourselves out of existence—for no one can make sense out of the human penchant for overpopulation. Faster and faster come the condos, the trailers, the malls, mass shelters for the kids of yesteryear—now with kids of their own. At some point, it will all come tumbling down, like the last, lost empire of the crows.

The demise of Mister Meadows brings to mind the death of another meadowlark, many years ago. I must have been ten, and "bows and arrows" were just beginning to be popular, both as toys and—for a few rugged individualists—as hunting weapons. Missouri bois d'arc trees, which we called Osage orange or "bow dark" wood, furnished excellent bow wood, and many hunters made their own in those simple days before pulleys and cables made bow-shooting an engineering rather than an aesthetic experience.

I was nowhere near that good, though. So I fashioned a crude bow from a willow wand, strung it with binding twine, and created a crude arrow out of another willow twig and an old nail. With these I stalked the farm, twanging away at everything and nothing—as long as it wasn't past the thirty-foot range of my bow.

One morning, I rounded the barn and saw a meadowlark on a fence post, madly trilling her joy. Perhaps she had just left a new life in her nest, but the thought never entered my mind. Without thinking, I shot—and the rough arrow pierced her breast. With a last despairing shriek, she fell to the ground, dead.

And I, who had never meant to hit her, have carried that cruel picture with me ever since.

❧ ❧ ❧

T rains roar past its vine-hidden entrance daily, but it's unlikely that any of the trainmen know of its existence. Getting to it takes some doing and a strong pair of legs—whether you go over the top of the mountain and down, or climb up to it from the railroad tracks below. The old Ku Klux Klan cave near Lanagan, Missouri, has a sad and sorry history, so entwined with local folklore it's hard to tell where truth leaves off and fiction begins. But to me it doesn't matter; I love caves, and anything about them fascinates me. And this one had been a *prison* cave.

The cave is on private land now, and no tourists are allowed in it. This wise action has protected what is left of the primitive hole in the hillside, although local vandals have done a lot to harm it. When I was last there, three years ago, only one of the old square steel bars that had blocked the single hacked-out window still remained. The others had been broken or worked loose and, for no apparent reason other than destruction, stolen.

The Ozarks are loaded with caves, and probably ten times as many are unknown and unexplored as are familiar. The Ku Klux Klan cave fascinated me the first time I heard about it from Steve Parnell, a young Ozark native who is a pilot for Jones Truck Lines, so in the late spring of 1975 he took me to it. We went over the mountain, tearing our painful way through more brambles and thorns than I knew the Ozarks possessed. And, although they supposedly did not frequent the area any longer, I also kept an eye peeled for timber rattlers— they could've traipsed over from Arkansas on a summer's night. The climb was a vigorous one and we were practically in the cave before I even saw it, sliding face inward along a ledge that was none too wide.

"It was easier to get to, back when it was used as a prison," Parnell said, making a final small leap that landed him at the cave mouth. "They had a stairway built up the mountainside. It was also used in the Civil War—as almost every cave in these parts was."

On that occasion the cave was flooded with water and the muddy debris of heavy spring rains. Springs, never far from the surface in these hills, added their run-off—possibly the same springs that had once watered prisoners of war or captive blacks.

We left, but my brief look through the opening and one of the tiny windows hacked from rock convinced me that I wanted to return. Entering a cave without companions is foolhardy, but this cave was only a few hundred feet deep—actually just a huge room—and I would be careful to let friends know where I was going.

I took the "scenic route" the next time I hiked to the Ku Klux Klan cave—down the Kansas City Southern's rickety tracks, near the point of the latest KCS derailment. (The line has had many derailments in these parts in the past few years—a sore point with the people who live here.)

Along the tracks stood the graying bones of an old telegraph line, surmounted by the amber insulators that now fetch premium prices at bottle shows—not that these ever could. Over the years, kids with .22's had shattered them, a fact that makes me shed a bitter tear, for I treasure all things old. Even an old insulator has seen a lot of history. The poles themselves were little more than lattices for vegetation.

At the mountain's foot, standing on a steel rail, I scanned the over-growth for signs of the cave. It was so perfectly hidden it took long minutes of walking up and down, peering upward, before I saw a hint of an opening and began my climb.

The earth still wasn't completely dry, and I slipped and slid as I grabbed brush and small trees to pull myself upward. Half an hour of concentrated labor and I'd grunted to the top, where I sat down on the small ledge and drained half my canteen of water. Then I turned my attention to the cave.

Inside, it was huge—diminishing in the gloom, slanting upward like some great rough saucer from the main central depression that covered a thirty-foot-square living area. The cave looked as if it could hold about a hundred men all told, yet I'd heard that many more had been crammed into it during the Civil War.

Later, under the jurisdiction of the Klan, the cave served as a hold-ing jail for blacks—and a place for the primitive inquisitions of the KKK. Sometimes white men who beat their wives or were publicly drunk were also thrown in the cave, a blow to their pride in those days of segregation and persecution.

Whoever they were, prisoners of war, victims of the KKK, or drunken, wife-beating white men, their ghosts cried out to me from the muddy walls. The sickening smack of a rifle butt against some Northerner's skull. The soft, rain-like sound of a whip lashing a pris-oner's back. The cries of agony, the whisperings in the night, the slow realization that this was their final destination before death took them away from the chains and the barbaric behavior of the powerful over the powerless.

An old hand-dug trench spanned the cave's length. Once it had tapped a flowing spring, furnishing the only water supply—for washing, for bathing under the cold gaze of guards and others, for cooking the grits and occasional meat brought to men who, before long, were little more than animals.

Another trench, slanting towards the dim light brought by two hacked-out iron-barred windows, exiting near them, had carried feces and urine out and down the mountainside. The cave, despite countless smoky fires that have left their mark on the ceiling, was never warm. Caves remain a constant fifty to sixty degrees, with 100 percent humidity. Lung sickness had to be common among prisoners held there for long periods.

My eyes drifted toward the lopsided windows. Only a single square bar remained where once there were ten. Around that single bar I imagined a pair of hands. The color does not matter. They were human hands.

✻ ✻ ✻

We were coming back from a day-long trip to Silver Dollar City and had stopped to see the veterinarian, a close friend. No sooner was I out of the car than he pulled me aside, his face grave.

"I've got some bad news," Rick Wooden told me. "Buster is dead. He was killed by a truck. Your dad has been calling here trying to find you."

So died Buster, our saint bernard, led astray, as it turned out, by a bad companion. Tramp, a worthless old hound Dad had taken in (and who was an incurable—and apparently unkillable—car chaser) had introduced Buster to the delights of that sport. But where Tramp was lean and agile, Buster was huge and clumsy. His feet got in the way and pitched him headlong under the wheels of a truck to instant death.

Who has never owned a dog? I've owned many, going back almost forty years to the first one I remember—Johnny. Dad brought him home one winter day, a fuzzy, yipping bundle shaped something like a toy collie. He scurried under the wood stove, where he stayed until lured out with a pan of cold milk.

Johnny became an inseparable part of our lives. A fair-to-middling stock dog, he was useful on the farm. But like most rural dogs, he was inclined to roam. One day he never came home. I talked with friends, but none of them knew anything. Then one afternoon a week later a farmer drove into our place and spoke with Dad. After he left, dad told me, "Old Johnny's been found."

Old Johnny. Aging and half deaf, he had wandered into the path of a school bus up near the farmer's lane. There wasn't much left, because summer deals with the dead quickly and efficiently. But his buff-colored fur was recognizable. As I walked home, I cried for the first dog I'd ever owned—and my first real acquaintance with death in any form.

There have been other dogs, and as each came to the end of his days, I vowed the pain was too much—that I would never again have another dog. But something always happened to change my mind. Some callous person would dump a puppy on my land, or a good friend would beseech me to reduce a new-puppy population by at least one—and I was a dog owner again.

Times have changed greatly since my boyhood, and today pets can quickly become a luxury that is hard to afford. They tie you down, often more than children, and in a peripatetic profession like mine that presents problems. But when I married again and adopted my wife's two small children, it was dog time again. Enter Buster.

My wife's father saw Buster in a box with another puppy some lady was trying to peddle. The word *free* linked on the cardboard cinched it. "This is just what those kids need," he said, and Diane, unable to resist a bargain, agreed. They named him Buster on the spot, and if ever a name fit, that one did—he was huge even as a pup and looked like he could bust down anything he blundered into. Unfortunately, what he blundered into most in his happy puppy fashion was the children. But finally, he learned to plop down in the sandbox with them as they played, a great brown mattress of fur and muscle for them to bounce on.

When my first children were born, I made sure they had dogs as soon as they could comprehend that their lustrous black eyes weren't marbles to be grabbed. Dogs—most of them—take an awful lot of loving punishment from kids, and always come back for more. I also overcame a boyhood bias and added a couple of cats, learning to like the felines as well as the canines, and sometimes convinced cats were less bother. But then, cats couldn't bark at prowlers. Buster's bark, at the height of his glory, could've caused avalanches in Afghanistan.

My sons learned about life, and its counterpart death, as most of us do—through the death of the first dog I ever got them. Scruffy, who also matched his name to perfection, died of cancer at the age of four. Up to then I'd never known animals can die of malignancies just like humans. Somehow, the grim knowledge drew me closer to my pets.

Chris, my oldest son, wanted to know where Scruffy was on the day following his euthanasia.

"What do you mean, he's gone away?" he asked, his lips trembling.

"Not gone away, son—put away. We had him put to sleep because he was very sick and in pain. Scruffy is gone for good, Chris."

"Will he go to heaven?" he asked, in his seven-year-old way, parroting back what he'd heard of that wonderful place in Sunday school.

I made some vague answer calculated to ease his mind. Yet I, who am not religious, found myself wondering at the wisdom of man, who has appointed himself a heaven but left loyal and faithful animals out in the cold. I have known pets that had more soul than many a human—they start no wars, create no acid rain, dump no toxic chemicals.

When I told my wife that Buster was dead, she took it so calmly I was amazed. But the next morning, I looked out the kitchen window to see her sitting, solitary and slumped, in our yard swing. She was crying.

When I went out to her and held her, she wept, "I'll never have another dog, never."

Yes you will, Honey. Yes you will.

❀ ❀ ❀

It was an Ozark morning without equal. Blue haze hung in the hollers and curled among the oak and sassafras trees. Above a pasture shining with dew sat a sun as orange as a frost-bitten persimmon, and even my three rowdy sons were awed and silent as we drove along the two-lane highway near Tiff City, Missouri.

Then we topped a rise. And there in the road squatted the Ozarks' resident monster.

"Look at that, boys," I said, stopping the car and putting on the emergency blinkers. (No need in getting run over by some moon-shiner returning, hung over, from his appointed rounds.)

"What on earth is it?" asked Jason, my middle son.

"Some kind of turtle, that's for sure," said Chris, my oldest.

"I bet it's a baby ankylosaur," said David Daniel, my youngest at eight and a real dinosaur freak. "It's got tail spikes like an ankylosaur."

"It's an alligator snapping turtle," I said. "Early Missourians called it that because they thought it was a cross between a turtle and an alligator." I got out of the car. "We'd better move it before it gets run over."

A comic opera followed on that day in 1977 that the boys still talk about. The young snapper weighed only about eight pounds, but its squat, armored body and the spiked tail and back made it look anti-social indeed. When I reached for its tail to rescue it, the ungrateful critter leaped into the air, turned half around and went *swish, Clonk!* I barely yanked my hand back before the turtle's powerful hooked beak made contact with the space it had occupied.

I've been bitten by snappers, and they make an impression. So this time, I used extreme caution, circling the turtle like a boxer, ready to feint if necessary—then, at the strategic second, I'd zip in and deliver the goods. But the little rascal beat me to the punch, or at least the snap, every time. That occasioned much merriment among my boys, none of whom offered to help.

There was no traffic, so I kept on trying. The reptile would have none of it. If I circled, he circled, his stubby body looking for all the world like some miniature animated pillbox. If I reached for him, he struck with snakelike speed. So there we danced, a would-be Good Samaritan and an armored pie plate.

Finally, inspiration struck. I kept a small tarp in my car trunk. Hauling it out, I draped several thick folds over the hissing turtle, picked it up (Whap! Whap! under the canvas), and dumped the turtle over the embankment, where it quickly scurried off.

It was no small accomplishment. Any creature that can battle up evolution's ladder unchanged for two-hundred million years is one tough cookie.

Snapping turtles are native to North America, but indiscriminate killing (plinking with .22's by callous hunters) has decimated their numbers, and now the largest concentration of them is found in the Ozarks.

There are at least three types, but by all accounts the most fascinating is *Machrochelys temmincki*—the alligator snapping turtle. Folklore says that if one bites down on a digit, it won't let go till it thunders. Chances are, it just seems that long. But severed heads of snappers have been known to bite a stick as long as eight hours after removal from the body.

When turtle hunters during the Great Depression killed snappers for their delicious meat, the heart beat slowly among the discarded viscera for hours. It is the turtle's extremely slow metabolic rate, coupled with the ability to eat anything from carrion to caviar, that has made it such a durable animal.

Meat shortages during World War II brought "turtling" back as a business, and one Ozarkian, the late Earl "Turtle" Ivy, a red-haired pixie of an Irishman, shipped as many as five hundred snappers a week, live in wooden barrels, to Philadelphia restaurants. Turtles can live for extremely long periods without food or water, one reason they were often the sole source of fresh meat on old-time sailing ships.

I went turtling with Earl in 1978, wading sloughs and muddy ponds as well as river and creek shallows where the wily snappers would "hole up" in communal dens. Summer heat induces torpidity, so they aestivate—similar to hibernation among animals in winter. Once he had located a colony, Earl got down and rammed his hand in, groping for tails—since turtles go in frontwards.

"But once't I got hold of me a *backward* turtle," Ivy told me, "which means the silly bugger had turned around and was facing *out*. He took a piece out of me, what I mean! Here, you can still see the scar."

Turtle Ivy caught twenty-five snappers on that hunt, and the biggest weighed a hefty twenty-five pounds.

"The big 'uns is about all gone," he said. "Time was, you could ketch turtles weighin' fifty or sixty pounds right reg'lar. But they done been hunted down."

His eyes brightened as he remembered, and he added, "Once't my daddy and me caught one that weighed eighty pounds. We tied it to a bobwire fence, and danged if it didn't pull that fence down and was headin' straight back into the river with it when we caught up with it!"

The 707 banked slowly, a silver dart homing in on Tulsa International Airport. Earlier I had threaded the clutter from three years of construction ("Pardon Our Improvements") to come and meet my oldest son. I hadn't seen him in two years. He had been twelve then. Now, he was almost fourteen and a totally different boy.

Different?

I pondered as he came out the gate toward me.

Not so much in looks and size. He was handsomer than ever, with too-long hair, richly brown, and the fine dark eyes of his Armenian mother. He wasn't large for his age but had the compact frame of the smaller athlete. In California he had done well in soccer, and one of his dreams, he'd confided in letters to me, was to become a bicycle racer.

"I'm saving the money from my paper route," he wrote, "to buy a racing bike. But they cost a lot."

Then one night he had called from California. Frustration and anger weighted his voice. "Dad, can I come and stay with you?"

"You know you can, Son, if it's all right with your mother and stepfather."

Several discussions later, he joined me in the Ozarks and enrolled in school. He said he liked the hills and rivers and seemed to embrace the slow pace of life. Occasionally, however, a frown would cloud his features, or he would subside into a moody silence, lost in dreams and thoughts all his own. It was clear that at times he missed his two younger brothers and the California friends he'd made in the seven years since my divorce.

I tried to interest him in the things I knew and wrote about. He even accompanied me, without much interest, on a few assignments, sometimes talking a blue streak about little, then slipping back into silence. I worried about him, rolled in bed at night wondering how to reach him, enlist him in a new life that, to me, was a bright and lovely thing. I awakened him at dawn to watch a tangerine sun slice above the horizon. When the white ghost-mists the Ozarks are famous for appeared, I walked with him into the hollows, the two of us becoming vague outlines to each other as we breathed the fragrant wetness. To all such sights Chris responded dutifully, and I truly think he got some small measure of joy out of them. But something was still missing from his life and from mine.

One late fall day, I took him camping with Jimmy Dalton, a neighbor who raised trout, a skilled fisherman. We built a big fire from an old downed cedar to soften the crisp chill of evening. Stars gleamed like holes piercing blue velvet, with the universal light shining through. Chris, his still-thin California blood unused to such rigors, shivered even in his heavy coat. I went to the tent and brought back a blanket, which he clutched around him gratefully. I could see that he thought wintry camping was for the birds—penguins.

"Chris," Jimmy Dalton drawled at one point. "Y'gotta come by sometime and see my trout farm."

"How can anybody farm trout?" Chris asked with characteristic bluntness. After a moment he laughed. "Farming trout," he said. "Gee, that sounds funny."

Dalton grinned his easy-going grin. "Well, it is funny sometimes," he admitted. "These are market trout, not the kind you catch. 'Sides, around here crappie and bass are your two big choices. You ever been fishin'?"

Chris shook his head, and Dalton said, "Well, you come on by sometime and we'll fish Doc's pond. It's got a lot of bass, and there's even an old boat there to go out in."

Chris glanced questioningly at me, and I nodded. "Sure," I said, "I've been meaning to take you fishing, but it seems like I'm always on the run."

"Hell, Chilly, why don't you bust loose and come too? We'll load my cooler with pop and beer and fish the mornin' away." Grinning, he added, "You ain't never gonna have time—you gotta take time."

I thought a moment. It occurred to me, then, that I was as caught up as I'd ever be. Except for a story I owed Harper Barnes at the *Post-Dispatch,* I was home free, a rarity I meant to take full advantage of.

Next morning, as a cuticle of sun edged the oaks and sassafras of Doc's creekside property, the three of us shoved off in a fat plastic dinghy. The day before, I had given Chris a new rod and reel. He was delighted, practicing in the cold November evening until it got too dark to see.

The sun was well up before Jimmy recorded the first strike—a largemouth of about two pounds. Furious thrashing. Excited yells from Chris, who almost dropped his own rod. Jimmy played the glittering dynamo expertly, yet suddenly, inexplicably, the bass was off his hook and headed for parts unknown. Chris's disappointment was boundless. "That was the biggest fish I've ever seen," he moaned. "I bet I never get one half that size."

I had been making long, looping casts, using a plug, stopping when Jimmy got his strike. Now I began again. Perhaps six casts later, a silvery typhoon ripped the water and the fight was on. I had never seen anyone as excited as Chris, especially since he had never fished. "Wow, *wow!*" he yelled, hopping around so even the untippable dinghy threatened to flop over. The bass would go perhaps three pounds, but it would also go scooting away seconds later. My son was inconsolable.

"If you and Jimmy can't land any, what chance have I got?" he mourned. Jimmy grinned and told him to keep trying.

Sometime around midmorning, Chris's rod nearly tipped the water. In his excitement, he cried out, his face animated and flustered, his hands all thumbs. "Help me, Dad, help!" he shouted, but Jimmy and I just angled our rods off to one side and gave him as much room as the boat permitted.

"I can't get him! *I'll lose him!*" My son's voice held a mix of desperation and panic. The fish was good-sized, at least a three-pounder. We knew there were no obstacles in this pond. In short, he should have no trouble landing this one, which was as it should be. We knew also that his mind was roiling with the awful fact that Jimmy and I had let ours get away.

"He won't break that ten-pound line," drawled Jimmy.

"You've got clear water," I counseled. "No brush to hang you up."

"But he's getting away! Look at him! He's getting away!"

"Don't get shook," Jimmy said. "Get shook, and that fish'll know it. He'll feel the vibrations, or the ESP, or something. Be calm and cool and you'll collect him, I promise."

So it came to pass, although to Chris the fracas must have lasted a hundred years. Our watches showed five minutes—not bad for a three-pound bass.

As Chris labored to clean his fish, Jimmy took me aside. "That was OK, suggesting that we file our hooks down. No barbs, no fish. Chris mightn't have felt so hot if we'd landed fish and he hadn't."

"Well, it was his first time out."

"I'll bet you a batch of Eagle Claws it won't be his last," Jimmy chuckled.

On the way home, Chris suddenly burst out, "I can't wait to get Jason and David here this summer!" He looked at me. "Okay for me to teach my little brothers how to fish, Dad?"

Smiling at his becoming a teacher after just one outing, I said, "Sure." Then I added with quiet pride, "Son."

✝ ✝ ✝

I had seen him on many occasions, always seated in his wheel-chair, always surrounded by dogs. He lived with his family at the top of a bare hill—bare, that is, except for one solitary, ancient oak. The rest of the hill sloped down into an Ozark holler, brush-filled and, in the spring, flower-laden. Spring and summer brought a measure of beauty to this austere rock pile. But in winter, it looked like nothing so much as a giant termite mount standing in a godforsaken desert.

In my decade in the Ozarks, I'd known all the occupants of the hill. This family—and the son who sat in the wheelchair and yelped de-lightedly back at the ecstatic dogs—was the third to own a piece of real estate most of the folks living around it figured was worthless to begin with. They had given a phenomenal thirty thousand dollars for the hill, the tree, and the sagging, ancient house on its crest. Almost immediately they discovered that the well quickly went dry if water was consistently used out of it. Cost of new well: five thousand dollars.

The twenty-acre spot did produce a few wild blackberries, but even they were not as profuse there as they were in the surrounding countryside. Even so, these were hard-working folks, and they made the best of a bad bargain. They'd come to make a home in the Ozarks, and they set about cleaning out the old, abandoned wreck and trying to patch enough leaks to make it liveable.

They bought a trailer and anchored it atop the crest of the hill. They built a wide deck around the trailer, with a railing. The railing was to keep the big man in the wheelchair from plunging off the edge—and perhaps careening down the steep, rock-strewn hill to serious injury or death.

As did all the neighbors, I helped a bit here and there. And on one visit, as I was chatting aimlessly, preparing to leave, I seemed to feel a gentle warmth between my shoulder blades. I turned—and met the placid gaze of the man in the wheelchair. A smile suffused his face, and five adoring dogs lay at his feet. He continued to look at me with that gentle, insistent gaze—a gaze as blank and empty as snowfields in winter, and yet, somehow, an expressive gaze.

His lips moved. His mouth opened. A high, gurgling squeak, like that of a delirious happy infant, broke on the air. Instantly, the dogs were up, whining, eager, surrounding him, licking his face and his large, unused hands. I smiled at him, a bit uncertainly. The high squeal of joy came again, and again there was pandemonium from the dogs.

I turned back to my host and his other half-grown son. They acted as if nothing out of the ordinary had happened. I left feeling unaccountably good about myself, about things, about the world.

Years went by, for these would be my neighbors on the hill for almost five years. Three or four times a year, I'd trudge up the impossible hill (their trucks and cars howled and groaned, even with a running start, so steep was the dozer-gouged road) to say "Howdy." On most occasions, the big, dark-haired man, always clean, always shaved—sat on the deck in his wheelchair. Sometimes his big hands idly fondled bright, small toys. But mostly, he stared straight ahead as though surveying some inner kingdom that I could never know. Or perhaps inside his mind, as on a sheer white screen, fantastic and wonderful shapes whirled and turned and glowed and sang.

At such times, the only thing that could catch and hold his attention were the dogs—five of them, all kinds and sizes. Theirs was a strange and marvelous communion. Once I saw the dogs come to their feet like quivering statues, seemingly pulled erect as if by unseen wires, to stand like ready sentinels in front of the infant man they loved. The occasion was when the property owner came to collect his money.

"*Yeee! Yeee!*" squealed the man in the wheelchair, but now the sound was blank, a noise and nothing more, without the unshaped gaiety his voice usually carried. The property owner was met with the payment before he reached the top of the hill, and he turned back as he had come.

If the man had been able to stand, he would have been over six feet tall. He was very heavy, too—I knew from watching his aging parents help him from the chair to the bathroom, or to the table for meals, where much of what he ate ended up in his hair—a fact he greeted solemnly, and sometimes with concern, for doubtless he had been scolded for his behavior in the past. "Yeee?" he would say softly. "Yeee?"

Sometimes I wondered how much he understood, if anything at all. He was able to show emotion, that was apparent. The most uncanny thing about him, though, was his ability to leave almost anyone who saw him in a better way emotionally than when they'd first come round. At first I thought it was because, by contrast, we were all so much better off. Or were we? This man-child was happy all the time, and loved. There was rarely anything like sadness in his clear, brown gaze.

The family is gone from the hill now. It's vacant and bare except for the oak and the old shack. I miss their son and wish I could see him one more time, crucified by his wheelchair, his faithful disciples at his feet. But most of all, I wish I knew his secret.

Somehow he made that barren hill the brightest place to be.

✤ ✤ ✤

On a hot summer day in 1949, I got my baptism of fireworks. Since then, I've credited myself with one extra eye and an additional thumb, because Pyro, the god of Mania, almost took them away on that long-ago Fourth of July.

The experience was both sobering and saddening—the latter because, dang it, it meant our parents had some justification for their worries. Anyway, whether from short fuse or leaking powder, a huge firecracker went off as I held it gingerly between thumb and forefinger just prior to tossing it in an empty rain barrel. I'd done this before, and the hollow Boom! was most gratifying.

Luckily, I was holding the cracker down by my hip for an underhand toss and not in front of me. Of course I was an idiot to be holding it at all, but at fourteen my wisdom knew no bounds.

I lit the fuse. There was a terrific bang. Sparks and bits of paper flew past my eyes, and my hand went numb. With a yell, I headed for the kitchen, where Mom bandaged my hand with a torn rag smeared with Vicks salve—a kind of over-the-counter cure-all used by every rural family.

At first I feared to look at what I knew was hamburger, but at last I summoned the courage. My hand was blistered and dark from imbedded powder, but all of a piece, and the thumb wiggled.

"Now then," Mom said grimly, "why don't you go back out there and play the fool again?"

For about ten minutes, I considered giving up fireworks altogether. But patriotism overcame good sense, and anyway my hand was the mark of a wounded veteran. Boys my age asked to see the horror under the bandage and offered plunder for the privilege. Girls shrieked and turned away when, with masterful grimaces, I showed it. By evening, I was saturated with sympathy and loaded with loot.

The Fourth of July was the greatest of all days in the lives of rural kids. For one thing, our city cousins (fireworks were banned inside city limits) could only envy us. We shot our bombs and rockets off in the country, and as long as we didn't start any prairie fires, the sky was the limit. Besides, what was independence from pesky Redcoats without fireworks in frisky red coats?

The list of treasures was endless—Sky Devils, Pinwheels, Cherry Bombs, Vesuvius Fountains. Tent stands sprouted like army camps, manned by gum-popping high school girls in saddle shoes and short skirts. Oh, boy, were they ever short! Some went all the way up to mid-shin. Those stands attracted moon-eyed youths like magnets, but when it came to girls, I was retarded. I was strictly there to ogle the explosives.

And what a trove! Half of World War II seemed remodeled just for our joyful application. Zebra brand had a zebra on the package. Black Cat brand had a black cat on the package. Red Devil had . . . but you get the picture. Fancy ads were out. It was product that counted, and the colors would gladden a peacock's heart.

A favorite of all kids was an enormous red cracker that could have reduced them to hay in a second. Even the boldest among us feared to fondle these giants. We placed them under cans, or under anvils, or if especially fearful, we'd put them under trucks—always relieved when the only things they lifted were cans. These they blasted into the stratosphere.

Tamest of all were the sparklers, and of course our parents always suggested these. We groaned at spending good money for something so dull, although they weren't bad for starting grass fires. But parents, being bigger, prevailed—so a brisk underground trade in "the real stuff" sprang up.

"Hey ya, Billy," a kid would ask. "Y'got'ny Red Boomers?"

"Red Boomers!" I would yelp. "Well, wouldn't I like some, though! Who's got 'em?"

"Jimmy the Chaw's got a whole box. He's over at th' gas station."

I was off like a Roman Candle. Jimmy the Chaw, an unsavory young man with a tobacco-stained mouth, was just selling his last Red Boomer to a customer. Dang! Those giant crackers would wake a statue. Glumly, I turned away, but within a block I'd traded a prized pocketknife for two of the deadly things.

Red Boomers were squat, ugly, and faded red in color. Menace was written all over them, and they had cost more than one digit among the unwary. We felt—probably rightly—that we could blow ourselves to kingdom come with hardly any effort. This added to their charm. Secretly, we believed they were made from stolen construction dynamite—but of course, this was simply a delicious fantasy.

Go-Devils were another popular item. To light one of these shrieking demons and watch it chase someone was delightful indeed. When one zoomed up the pants leg of an athlete I was jealous of, I felt ashamed—for I saw at once why he was star material. Had there been a category called Trousers Removal, he could have taken an Olympic medal.

I still love the Fourth of July. It celebrates freedom, not war. It denotes a time when citizens stood up, made their voices heard, and weren't afraid to be counted. We've come a long way since, but don't seem so sure of our directions any more.

In 1982, my fifteen-year-old son Chris went with some other boys, and they started shooting off fireworks. A Vesuvius Fountain went off in his face, causing second-degree burns. For weeks he was coated with Silvadene ointment. Miraculously, he emerged with only minor scarring.

Now, on any Fourth of July that my sons are with me, ol' Dad supervises the whole celebration. They may squawk a bit at not getting to light anything but sparklers, but boys know they can count on a good show.

On all ten of their fingers.

❀ ❀ ❀

3

It could be a blue lagoon,
this small pool on Buffalo Creek,
and the children bronze platoons
of a people who once made

arrowheads here. See the sleek
young mothers as they wade,
skirts bunched among the wild
onions; see the babies splashing

in the shallows. Swimmers watch
as the sun rests in a mountain notch
and the creek comes alive
with kids racing for one last dive.

It's Tom and Huck and Becky again,
here in these Ozark shallows,
watched by the ghosts of Indians
in the blue haze of the hollows.

I was halfway home from the Tulsa airport when a sense of loneliness and desolation suddenly overwhelmed me. Turning off the Will Rogers Turnpike onto a road devoid of weekend traffic, I pulled over and started to weep—great, splashing silver tears that just kept coming.

They were gone, my summer sons, gone back to their other home, their main home, the one they had occupied ever since a California judge decreed that they should stay with their mother, ten long years before.

In those years, I saw them infrequently. Like animated film frames, they seemed to leap upward in growth each time I saw them. Chris, now seventeen, and a handsome boy. Jason, fourteen, and an "all around nice guy" to his peers. David, twelve, trying but often failing to keep his turbulent emotions under control. Chris had stayed home to look for a summer job, so I had only the two younger boys—and this had been their first trip to the Ozarks in two years.

From the first day, they had banged against my hermit-like existence like pebbles in a tin can. Soon my jangled nerves were prompting me to yell at them, telling them to be more considerate, to pick up their dirty socks, to help with the housework, to—for God's sake!—*shower* once in awhile. Did I have to lead them to everything and make them do it?

My shouts echoed in my mind now, as I sat beside an Oklahoma highway trying to cut short this silly crying—which could not bring them back in any case. I looked up at the sky, although the plane carrying them to Oakland was probably even now landing in Dallas. They had flown only once before.

"What do we do in Dallas, Dad? How will we know what plane?" Jason had asked.

"I'll ask the airline to help you, son," I said. "They'll most likely assign someone to take you to your next flight when you change there in Dallas."

"I just hope I don't forget my cassette player," said David fervently, for he meant to take it aboard as seat luggage.

And so, there at Tulsa, they were ticketed, tagged, and told their gate number. We got there more than an hour early, yet the time flew past. A few video games on the floor above, a few surprised utterances at an ancient biplane strung by wires from the ceiling—and we were passing the search gate and joining the throngs walking toward Gate 25.

I was born in and spent some of my life in Oklahoma. I've always been at war with my native state to the extent that if such things were possible, I'd have my birth state legally changed to Missouri. Oklahoma must not appeal much to its writers and artists, because almost all of them have fled from its red dust as fast as they could.

But today, perhaps brightened by the salt water in my eyes, Oklahoma—this part at least—had a shimmering green quality that made it far prettier than I had ever seen it. They call the northeastern section "Green Country." This day it was, although often it's about as green as a dirt dauber's clay nest.

As I sat there, a tiny steel-enclosed speck on a vast prairie, the horizon stretched like some earthbound sky, or like a reflection of the bowl above it. Purple lilac-shaped clouds sprouted from the horizon. *When lilacs last on the skyline bloomed.* . . .

The emptiness of the prairie equaled my own. Lord, how I missed my sons. But only hours before I'd been on their backs to make sure they had everything; to forget no clothes, no toys, no tapes. "Get it all!" I hollered. "Look under your beds, look everywhere!" Inside me, I knew the main reason was so I could make a clean break again, as so often in the past.

Finding items left behind produced the children, almost the smell and heat of them, their hurt eyes when ol' Dad came down too hard on them, their own anger and frustration as they tried to understand a father first, a writer second—neither of them all that great.

If an Oklahoma highway patrolman had come along then, what a shock he would have had, finding a middle-aged, overweight man in overalls with red eyes and a blue bandanna on the dash in front of him.

Well, they had seen worse. I started my pickup, made a U-turn on the deserted pavement and headed back to the turnpike. The lilac clouds had increased and were larger as well as being a deeper purple. Switching on the radio, I heard tornado warnings being issued. The daily dangers of all our lives went on.

There are times when I wonder what parent birds feel when their fledglings leave the nest—whether it is genuine pain or simply the mindless orchestration of some instinct.

We humans have judges to rule our lives. For good or ill, we usually do what the state tells us to. As for what it may do to our kids, that's for the future to show. There are no easy decisions in such things—just decisions.

My sons are doing me proud, so far at least. I think of them often, but there's little point in brooding. Or in feeling guilty because I wasn't around when being around might have made a difference. As I look back, I think my being there might have made the difference a bad one. I'll never know, nor will my sons. Besides, there's always next summer.

Back home I fell to cleaning the trailer. In short order, I had found a bathing suit, a shirt, and a sock—all much too small to be mine.

In the Ozarks, spring comes in on little calf feet, but fall comes in on thunder.

Nothing I know is as awesome as a full-fledged autumn storm, with winds near hurricane force, tree limbs breaking and falling, cows huddling nervously under trees for shelter against the pelting rain.

Not long ago, a local farmer went out into his pasture after a storm and found thirty-three prize Holsteins dead around the base of a giant oak. Lightning had struck the tree, and the wet cows, perfectly grounded at four points each, all absorbed the killing bolt. I can still see the picture that ran in the local paper—cows strewn in a circle around the tree, as though they had simply lain down for a nap. And forty thousand dollars worth of dairy stock was dead by an act of God.

Ozark storms are a way to welcome winter—although winter is rarely welcome to farmers who must stockpile hay, rafters high, to feed livestock when snow flies. Dad tells me that the average Missouri farmer keeps thirty-five to forty cows. His thirty-five will eat a thousand to twelve hundred bales of hay—roughly fifty thousand pounds—unless winter is especially hard. Then other sources for hay must be found.

Dad raises about half his hay, and when baling time comes around he scans the skies every day, hoping there will be no rain. Hay is mowed, left to dry, and then baled—and if rain comes before it is baled and stowed, some of it will rot, and all of it will be reduced in quality.

It is common practice for farmers to sell off quantities of animals before winter, so they won't have to feed them. In theory, this is the time when beef should be cheapest, because the farmer himself is the victim of the selling glut. But cheap meat at the market isn't always guaranteed—in the winter or anytime.

Some urbanites have long since learned to adapt rural ways to city life. Farmers will usually take a beef, hog, or both to local family-size slaughterhouses. There, the animals are butchered and packaged for the deep freeze at prices considerably lower than those in the supermarket. Some city dwellers buy freezers, then go to the country and buy their animal on the hoof. It's a little more work, but for considerable savings—and such beef is generally better than beef that has been in feeding pens awaiting shipment, in some cases being fed steroids or other chemicals to add flesh.

Autumn storms bring a variety of ills to small stock farmers. They must spot likely erosion spots and fill them in with rocks or debris, and they must keep an eye out for calves that might drown in rushing creeks or swollen rivers.

During one incredible storm a few years back, I was canoeing with three friends. We'd camped on a high bluff overlooking Arkansas's White River—and when dawn came, water was already lapping at the ledge. The tethered canoes were still intact, so we loaded gear and shoved off—into a heaving muddy sea that had once been a river.

We made it across, by the grace of good fortune, but what sticks most in my mind is the image of a full-grown cow, turning slowly over and over in the brown flood. First belly, with swollen, distended udder, then spine and horned head, then poker-stiff legs thrust rigidly toward heaven, as if in bovine protest that such a fate had befallen her.

The Ozarks flex their muscles during the fall storms, and those who hike, canoe, or camp during this time of flaming leaves and turbulent waters must be ready for anything. (For all I knew, on that stormy day, there were humans rolling in the river as well, down toward the bottom, bouncing off submerged trees, their eyes forever closed with river silt.) And I don't mean just amateurs—more than one Ozarks expert has found himself outwitted by the woods, hills, and waters of Missouri and Arkansas. Death by Ozarks is more impersonal than a slaying in a St. Louis alley—but the end result is the same.

I'm probably crazy, but I love violent storms. Often I have stood on my exposed deck, a bearded Ahab roaring at the gale, feeling the rain vaccinating my face, feeling the powerful winds buffeting my aging tin box of a home. I feel closer to nature, which serves as my deity, at such times.

❉ ❉ ❉

Each of our lives parallels the encroaching seasons, which suck our green juices and leave stalks dry as cereal. I see the old, old men, seated in the patience age brings, watching the morning sun and the winter rain from porches of old folks' homes.

That's what we called them when I was young. But now as I slowly edge towards their plateau, they're called other things—bureaucratic names like "senior citizens facilities" or small town names like "rest homes." Nothing, however, can change the changing seasons that pull us like magnets towards that last, great adventure.

Knowing that has rendered me more philosophical in my middle years—but it's still an uphill battle to be the kind of person I'd like to be. Sometimes wittingly, sometimes unwittingly, I still hurt those I share the planet with. With every passing year, though, I find mellowness that wasn't there when I was wild and young.

Take the time twenty-five years ago when, on an abandoned runway in Florida, I laid straight out on my motorcycle seat and cranked the throttle until the engine screamed at the torture it was undergoing. The speedometer needle knocked at 100, 110, 120—finally flailing against the peg, unable to go further even as the engine wound and wound and wound. I had to be going at least 130 miles an hour, straight as a stick, alone on a Harley with no one to pick up the shattered bones and torn flesh if I hit so much as a pebble. Such was my foolishness because a girl had broken up with me.

I've often realized that my bones should've been interred many years ago, for I've been luckier than some I've known. The risks I've taken—and still take—have seemed to say something for me, to be a loud announcement to the universe that I lived, lived, *lived*.

And now that I'm teaching one of my sons to drive, I want him to go slow, slow, *slow*. The paradox of parenthood: Don't do as I do, do as I say. And our kids will likely say it to their kids.

In Anderson, catercorner from the funeral home but several houses away, there is a place where old folks live. It's called a "boarding home," a name I love for its softness, its humanity, its recognition that those therein aren't just pieces of meat. The name implies that even advanced age can bring with it that spirit of independence that marks my own father, whose failing health has not yet made him want to leave his ramshackle house and beloved cows to sit and watch the sun.

He can still watch the sun from the cracked concrete slab of his own roofless porch, in the glittering presence of a great, bright maple tree. But none can read the future—and someday he may find a boarding home of his own—not the cold, efficient government kind, but one staffed by caring people, who know Dad's children will be watching.

I am a wedge driven between generations—our middle years make us such—and comparisons are hard to avoid. When I was a kid, I took for granted the snow-haired grandma who lived with us, shelling peas on the porch while she rocked slowly towards eternity. I still see her in my mind, though now the face has blurred—for she has been a phantom forty years. My grandma never lived in an old folks' home.

Not long ago, held like a pea in the steel pod of my small car, I gripped the wheel tensely while cars and trucks roared around me on a St. Louis freeway. I thought of all the fragile lumps of flesh operating those vehicles, each taking for granted that their machines would work well, and not kill them that day.

I thought of all those folks, hurrying, hurrying, hurrying—as if they had some place to go besides the place that waits for all of us at the end of the freeway of life.

※ ※ ※

Nights have a special magic in the Ozarks, and it doesn't matter what time of year it is.

One recent midnight, I stepped outside, feeling the crispness of fall in the air and drinking in the sounds and sights as I had done so many times before.

Could I ever leave this place? The days brought their share of worries and woes, just as they did for folks in the city. But darkness washed the slate clean, a midnight laundry preparing the world for the next sunrise.

A wind was blowing, the kind that makes the treetops talk and flips the flying bats as if they are falling leaves. And over it all, the steady shrilling of bugs and frogs, each tucked in some crevice or hidden under some rock. Their little worlds, too, were hidden by darkness.

Almost every farm in the Ozarks has a tall pole, topped with a mercury vapor light that burns until dawn, then switches off automatically. Invented as deterrents to thieves, they also possess a beauty of their own—especially when their tall stalking shapes are circled by trees. Then the lamp, made flickery by leaves, casts tiny golden eyes on the porch and sides of the house—like a revolving mirror-ball in some long-ago dance hall.

The mercury light in my yard cast a moonlight glow, so that walking took some getting used to. There was a point at the edge of the house where it was as gloomy as the dark side of the moon, and a hidden roof or rock could have tripped me up.

The place changes at night, becoming *terra incognita*—unknown territory—and I spanned the centuries backward to become a Spanish explorer, moving carefully forward into a strange land. Vines rasped like nesting cottonmouths as they drooped from the trees. The grass was thick and matted, braided with a few wild flowers that looked weak and pale because there had been no rain.

Then a different light was seeping into the yard's dark side. I looked to the east—and saw a sight of such beauty it took my breath away. A moon of golden amber was edging over the dark line of trees. Soon it was above them in the velvet sky, a medallion hanging from the throat of heaven.

The wind increased, its low moans barely audible above the racket from the woods north of the house. How dark it was beneath their branches, like some never-ending cave luring me in.

Here, the dangers of falling increased. I stayed close to the edge of the woods, where some of the light still penetrated, making my way toward an old familiar sitting place—the huge, iron-hard trunk of a walnut tree Dad had taken out of the grove in order to dig the well and make room for my trailer.

The tree, bleached white by years of rain and sun, had lain in this spot since 1973. Wild roses had grown up around it—a scourge to be hacked down, for they have thorns but no blossoms. Countless small animals had sheltered under it, pausing on some journey of their own. The tree reposed like the thigh bone of some long dead monster. I sat down on it and looked back at the light, the night-sun of my humble world, at the cloud of insects swirling around it—at the tumbling bats that raid like winged sharks.

It's not a bad analogy. Night in the Ozarks is a sea lapping quietly at the edge of creation. What covered me then had hidden the terrible dinosaurs. The moon bobbing like a golden boat had shone on countless scenes of life, death, birth—and the mindless music of ten thousand singing insects.

The magic and the mystery.

I'd better enjoy them while I can.

Already there are men planning mines in the solitude of national forests.

Already the forces of greed and rapine are gathering to mangle these silent hills.

❀ ❀ ❀

When two of my three sons visited the Ozarks this past summer, I saw a chance to bone up on my education. Lost as I was in the world of ordinary conversational English, there was little chance of my understanding what they talked about unless I got on their wavelength. For lack of a better word, I'll call their utterances "Teenspeak"—and I'd need a year in a Berlitz school just to understand the nuances.

But let me befuddle you. One of the first things I did when my sons and I had got reacquainted was to have a splendid blitzer, at which we munched and guzzled until you could gag me with a spoon.

"Wow," I kept saying, "Is this gnarly, boys?" For I am nothing if not quick on the uptake. Only this uptake was wrong, apparently, for both burst out laughing.

"Not gnarly, Dad," Jace said. "More like awesomely cool!"

"Yeah," David added enthusiastically. "It's bad, Dad—a real killer!"

About then a young dude came and said, "What's up?"

"Hey, nothin's happenin'," Jason said—despite the fact that a lot was happening all around us. "You scope out any fine chicks yet?"

"Chicks!" I yelled. "Hey, you guys still say chicks? We said chicks when I was a kid!"

All three looked at me strangely, but ignored my outburst. The lad walked away, probably to scope out some fine chicks.

"Man, he's massive," David said admiringly. "He's no punk rocker, new waver, or stoner though. And he's too cool to be a loner."

"You got it," Jace said. "Mess with him, and you're dust."

"He's no preppie, schoolboy, or teacher's pet either," said David.

"Teacher's pet!" I hollered. "Hey, we used teacher's pet when I was a kid!"

"You can just tell he's a real stud," said Jace.

"Radical," my youngest son agreed. "A bad dude."

"Boys," I said. "Did I ever tell you what dude meant when I was your age? They had these ranches, see, out in Arizona and places. And the tourists that went to them were called dudes on account of they weren't real cowboys, see, and . . ."

"Cowboys?" Jace said. "Who's talking about cowboys, Dad? Oh, by the way—it wasn't cool to answer you when you asked about chicks. I mean, here was this killer and we were talking to him, and it was real gnarly of you to just butt in like that."

"You're absolutely right," I said miserably. "I'm sorry. But tell me, do you still say chicks when you mean women?"

"No, just when we mean girls," David said.

"But doesn't that upset any young feminists?" I asked.

"Oh, we don't go out with libbers," Jace said. "Nobody dates them, Dad."

"That sounds awfully mean."

"Us mean?" David laughed. "You ought to see *them!* We just don't want the hassles. We treat them like they treat us. If they want to be loners, and treat us like homeboys, we've got a right to pick whoever we want to."

Ah, me, here was society in microcosm, the battle of the sexes almost before sex was an issue—and in an enlightened California city at that. For my sons lived near San Francisco.

"Fine chicks aren't libbers, Dad," Jason said candidly. "Bad dudes want fine chicks, and fine chicks want bad dudes. Was it any different when you were a teenager?"

I thought back to Cookie, Snookums, Patricia, and Jean something-or-other, all females from my 1940s past. Of them all, Patricia was the most beautiful. I never had a prayer with her, mainly because all the bad dudes were scoping out the fine chick that she was.

Yes sir, it paid to be a handsome athlete when it came to Pattie. She probably never knew that a skinny tow-headed runt longed to write her a poem and leave it in her locker. Not only did a cast-iron caste system reserve beauties like her for the jocks, but Pattie probably wouldn't have given a fig for a poem from a nerd. Her killer owned a car.

Well, love hurts, it sure does, and both sexes feel the pain. Jean what's-her-name was passionate for me—as passionate as ninth-graders can be—but alas, she was no beauty. I wasn't, either, but then I wasn't trying to date myself. And Jean came after me like she meant it, which kind of scared me off.

"Well, boys," I said, coming out of my reverie, "I guess things were much the same when I was your age. But maybe it's harder to know how to treat females these days. Even so, it doesn't hurt to be considerate of others' feelings—even if your own get hurt in the process. You know, it's very hard to be a woman."

"Is it harder than it is to be a man?" David asked.

I looked at their fresh young faces. Life had yet to leave its signature there, but it would. It would be their tough teacher, as it had been mine. I pondered the question, innocent but so complex. In all my fifty-one years I had never faced it head-on, much less answered it. Now, for my sons, I did.

"Yes, boys," I said, "I think it is."

As part of a St. Louis Symphony fund-raiser, I was sold down the river.

I inquired as to who had bought my ticket, since a few folks would buy it just to boil me in oil—the kind drained from old crankcases. "The Dierbergs," I was told. Because I'm not from St. Louis, I asked my editor if they were friendly. He said yes, and that the Dierberg family owned supermarkets in and around St. Louis.

What a piece of luck! By chance, I had just completed a course at the Acme Consultant School. Here was my chance to be of some help to my hosts—free, of course. Brand-new ideas for their supermarket chain were already churning in my skull when, for research purposes, I visited the Bogey Hills Plaza store in St. Charles (Coleridge's poem "Kubla Khan" describes this market in the opening lines: "In Xanadu did Kubla Khan / A stately pleasure-dome decree.")

As I wandered glittering aisles laden with every kind of merchandise, from imported foods to family magazines, I couldn't help admiring progress, which until then, I had been suspicious of. Even the checkers were happy under their hollowed, scrolled domes above the registers. "Do you like working here?" I asked the lady who took my money, and she allowed as how she certainly did, while giving me a strange look.

But a few vital items were lacking, and in so fine a place their absence made them stick out like unshined shoes. When a friend and I met with Roger and Barbara Dierberg for dinner, I took their measure and they took mine. Although neither of them was wearing overalls, they were neatly dressed—and Barbara Dierberg's easy humor put us at ease. Roger's keen, direct gaze and firm handshake told me that here was a man whose mind was always open to new ideas.

"Roger," I said as we sat down, "I've just been to one of your markets, and you have a problem." I gave him my card. It was quietly simple, with the red ink muted and the green edges just the right shade. He admired it a moment before pocketing it.

"Ever since your grandpa started the business in 1914, you've constantly expanded and tried new marketing techniques—right?"

"Yes, we have," Roger admitted. Meanwhile, Mrs. Dierberg and my friend were chatting about stuff on their own.

"Well, then," I said—and paused for effect—"where are the possums?"

"What?" Roger Dierberg appeared startled.

"Possums, man. You're missing a big market in Ozark pets. Push possums, Roger, and profits will soar."

"But we already have banks, post offices, and florists in our stores . . ."

"And delis?"

"Of course," he said. "They're one of our most popular features."

"I can't understand why," I said. "At the one I visited, there was a complete lack of barbecued raccoon and fried snapping turtle."

Dierberg was looking a bit dazed, so I eased up. A good consultant can afford to be gracious. After all, he's there to help his client, and getting the client confused is only part of it.

"Here's how I see it," I said. "If Dierberg's wants exotic foods, the Ozarks are chock full. Why, we have snails down there that would eat Frenchmen. Salamander steaks are available, if you know the right poachers. And gar! My gosh, they're practically an untapped resource! Just think of the revenue you're missing."

I'd gotten so wound up, I hadn't noticed I was talking to myself.

"They had to leave," my friend said sourly. "I'm sure you know why."

"I certainly do. They're going to start immediately to import the stuff I mentioned from the Ozarks."

"Whatever gave you that idea?" my friend snapped, as we left.

"I may be a consultant," I said smugly, "but I am also a customer. Customer is just another word for king, my dear. Mark my words, it's just a matter of time until they start paying attention to my ideas. Why, I might even bring some trained possums and put on a show."

My friend didn't hear. She had pulled her collar up.

❧ ❧ ❧

The cream-colored bulldog looked like a nailkeg, so swollen was she with puppies she could not give birth to. Fifty years ago she would have been doomed, but on this day the local vet had her on his stainless steel operating table, knocked cold by narcotics in preparation for a Caesarean section.

Vets are some of my favorite people, and I fear I sometimes overdo the welcome they extend to me. But until they chase me out with a scalpel, I mean to keep on a-comin'. And besides, we were under a tornado watch. My tin-topped Hilton wasn't nearly as safe in high winds as the Anderson Animal Hospital, which was constructed of cement blocks.

As the wind keened shrilly at the O.R. window, Dr. Wooden made a long central incision down the bitch's midsection. (Legend has it that Julius Caesar's ancestor was born *a caeso matris utere*, "cut from the womb of his mother," thus originating the operation over two thousand years ago. But few were done before modern anesthesia came along.)

"Holy mackinaw," the vet said, carefully lifting innards from the unconscious bulldog. "It's a baby factory in here." One by one, over a period of half an hour, he drew forth and clamped the umbilicals on nine puppies, passing them to his wife, Peggy, and his assistant, Carol Sampson, for resuscitation. Soon the O.R. was filled with new-puppy yips and wails. With amazing volume for such tiny things, they tuned up like a Chinese orchestra.

The owners, however, were not happy. They raised dogs—a big business in the Ozarks—and had one of the finer kennels. They had artificially inseminated their bulldog bitch, but a golden Labrador retriever had put in his bid earlier—thanks to a broken door—and only one of the pups would fetch the usual $350 brought by its pedigree.

The vet had come in on a Sunday to save the dog's life and had spent two hard hours in prepping, surgery, and cleanup. Yet he felt so sorry for the kennel owners, he charged them less than what the operation was worth. But I don't wish to paint veterinarians as saintly folks. My doctor would probably do the same—and when I give birth to nine pups, I bet he will.

The wind had picked up its tempo—and when I stepped out of the building, it was to a return to the dustbowl days. I had been a small boy when much of Oklahoma, Texas, and New Mexico filled the skies. Now here they were again, an eerie and frightening reminder of the stupidity of certain people in regard to our topsoils.

Many times I had watched the bulldozers of real estate developers ripping out trees on hillsides—which became rutted and ugly red long before the first "vacation cabin" was built. But no one seems able to stop these soil destroyers for long, even though it is just as easy for them to protect the earth by more careful development—as opposed to the runaway greed that motivates many of them.

Still, it's not fair to single out the developers. Here in the Ozarks, musical acres is quite a game. I know farmers who've gladly sold part of America to the Arabs, Japanese, and other foreign interests—who can then do what they wish with it. No doubt people do the same thing in other countries. The bright spot is that if we do it enough, we may become one world and get along better.

The sky had been a burnished copper when I came into town. Now it was a sullen amber, while the sun was only a pale disk barely visible through the wind-borne dust. Ah, Missouri! Just one week before we had been squishing through enough water to green the Mojave. Now we were blowing in the wind.

Six miles later I pulled into Dad's driveway. He was barely visible, bent to the cold, howling wind, wrapped in a brown caul of dust as he stumbled towards the chicken house with a coffee-can full of feed for his new baby chicks.

"Where ya been?" he hollered. "I tried t'call ya—the electricity is out."

I explained in the hen house, out of the wind, then asked if he'd ever seen anything like this in Missouri before.

"Not this bad," he said. "Hell, that's most o' Mexico up there."

Dad remembers the dustbowl days vividly, when days passed with no sun visible, or when at best only a pale acetylene spark pierced the dull bronze skies. There are places to this day where dust piled so high in the 1930s that the tops of buried, rotted buildings can still be seen sticking out of the earth.

A huge limb had fallen, blocking one road home. I turned back and took another. At the trailer, I'd cracked my windows against storm pressures before leaving—and now the place was full of dust. Well, what better way to visit several states without going anywhere?

The wind was dying. The sky was a pale, lovely shade of tangerine. The radio told me that one of the Almighty's tornadoes went to church in an Oklahoma town and took away a worshipper.

The electricity was still off. I took down my old kerosene lamp, feeling strangely like I was living once more on the Oklahoma plains, in a sharecrop shack, listening to the wind, watching the dust, counting the days until I was old enough to escape.

🜚 🜚 🜚

T hor is at it again, rolling his iron carriage across heaven, throwing his hammer and striking fire—sending messages of thunder to the hills below. Never mind that he is a Norse god and this is the Ozarks. A good god should not be wasted, and this one heralds the aging of autumn. Trees bend like summer grass as the wind hits. No artillery can equal the sustained sound of a late fall storm.

The rain is on the march—but march or not, I must hie me to Anderson before the market closes. Somehow, lost in my paper world, I've run out of rations.

Wombulla, wombulla, woooomm. . . .

Lightning filigrees the dark sky with traceries of silver—a heavenly embroidery that surely awes the angels. Black clouds scud past overhead. A widowmaker, long overdue to fall, crashes to the floor of my small forest, frightening a calf who breaks for the pasture and the safety of the herd. I wonder if Dad is heading for the storm cellar over at his place.

Inching the car out the gate, I move down the tunnel of trees that always makes the lane so magical at night. Headlights carve ghostly sculptures from brush and trees. Their limbs thrash wildly, like the tentacles of some mythical beast.

That old Ozark magic's got me in its spell,
That old Ozark magic that I know so well.

Time has got away again, spinning around the platen of my IBM. It had been a busy day. A lawyer from St. Louis, driving through, stopped to chat. Two elderly travelers came later to talk with me about the Ozarks.

"When are you going to write a book?" the latter asked.

I told them I hope it is soon and waved them on their way.

Just past Pleasant Grove Church, with its lonely tower beseeching god to be there for humankind's ever-mounting needs, a sodden toad flops across the asphalt. In the glare of my headlights, the rain looks like wires strung from some heavenly harp. No night to be out, but a favorite for me. I'm a storm junkie.

So powerful is the wind that it turns raindrops into tumbling bullets. The tiny missiles veer and yaw, as though chasing some unseen enemy—rain rockets blasting so hard they make my wipers falter.

The lightning has become steady pulses of light now. The constant firing gives the wiper blades the illusion of being multiplied. It's the stroboscopic effect; quick, bright flashes that make rotating objects jerk as they move. Wind, rain, roadside oaks in a helpless ballet— these are why I love night driving in Ozark storms.

The rain has filled the roadside ditches. Brown water seethes between grassy banks, spills over the road in low places, and races headlong toward Elk River, Buffalo Creek, Big Sugar, Little Sugar, and finally to Grand Lake across the Oklahoma line.

Then, as suddenly as it came, the storm is gone. The wind dies. The scudding clouds turn to fish scales, lighten, swim on to the east toward St. Louis. Stars start to appear, glittering like insect eyes, and the crispness of an autumn night is once more with me.

Near town, the red tail lights of cars headed for the local movie merge with Highway F from side roads—parents going to pick up their kids.

They are so pretty in the silent darkness. Like distant necklaces strung together. Like rubies dancing through the night.

※ ※ ※

I have been in love, and so have you. I can remember the pain, and so can you. There is no pain like that of a love that has gone bad, or that you want but cannot have—or that you lose to death. And all we have to counterbalance it are the moments of joy.

A long time ago, a special woman brought such moments to me. She came to the Ozarks from an Eastern city to spend Thanksgiving with me in my trailer. The four days we would have together were to be our last—a fact she knew better than I. For even then, her rampaging cells were murdering her.

I had met Gloria on a plane headed for Panama, where I was going to do a magazine story about our astronauts and their jungle survival training. She was small, pretty, and had hair so black it was almost blue. Her eyes were large and dark, and she told me she was a high school teacher. I told her I was a free-lance writer.

"What do you write?" she wanted to know.

"Anything that pays the rent," I said, and then added: "I've published a couple of books of poetry. Slim volumes of forgotten verse."

I struck a pose as best I could in the airplane seat, and she laughed at my martyred expression.

"Just be thankful you can write," she said. "I've always wanted to be a writer, but I just don't have the ability. You're very lucky that you do."

Back in the Ozarks, a letter was waiting. "Dear Chilly," Gloria wrote. "I went to the library and read some of your poems and stories in old copies of the *Southern Review*. I just wanted to write and tell you that it's nice to know somebody famous!"

Thus began a correspondence that lasted until 1980. In her third letter, Gloria mentioned that she had been going to a doctor for tests. Sometime later she wrote, "I didn't tell you when we first met, but I had been having some health problems. I thought everything was under control, but I guess it wasn't. I'm off work for awhile. If you don't object, I'll visit you in the Ozarks for Thanksgiving."

I had a motorcycle then, and Gloria clung to me like a burr as we roared into the walls of wind, wild and free as two blown leaves. All the things about the Ozarks that I loved, she loved. Her eyes sparkled in the crisp November air—and somewhere in a hidden hollow, stopped for a picnic, we saw something fine in each other's eyes.

That night she said, "Please don't look." Her voice was small and sad, and when I reached to hold her in the dark, I knew why. Gloria had had a double mastectomy.

"I didn't know how to tell you," she wept.

"You didn't have to tell me anything," I said, holding her tightly against me.

There's a poem by James Dickey called "Cherrylog Road," about two kids who ride a motorcycle into an abandoned auto graveyard, and in those improbable surroundings discover love for the first time. My favorite lines are: "I held her and held her and held her, / Wild to be wreckage forever."

Our last days were like a poem, so much in so small a space, and when I left Gloria at the airport on Sunday, the blue November day shriveled and died. It was weeks before a letter came, and in it, almost as though she was already detached from life, Gloria wrote that doctors had found a metastasis of the liver.

"I'm on an experimental drug that seems to help," she wrote. "However, in January he found new problems in my bones, and now I'm taking double-doses of two anti-estrogen drugs to try to avoid chemotherapy, which looms out there in the future."

She added: "On the positive side, I'm grateful that my school insurance is such that I don't have to return to work while I'm ill like this."

Gloria never said so, and never indulged in self-pity, but I knew she suffered great pain, nausea, and weakness from the drugs and radiation treatments. I asked if I could come and see her. She refused. On June 11, 1980, she wrote her last letter to me.

"The past few weeks have been relaxed and peaceful. I keep planning to do great and wonderful things, but energy, which I once had in abundance, seems to be lacking. I have to tell you that my doctor and I had a 'hard facts' talk. He said that barring any new complications, the best prognosis I could hope for would be five years."

Gloria died a year later.

❧ ❧ ❧

Sometimes in the Ozarks, a life can be saved that seemed almost certainly lost.

I had just finished cooking breakfast and getting Jason off to school when there came a banging at the door. The door opened and Dad walked in.

I invite Dad here a bunch, both because it's good for him to stare at other walls than his own and because sometimes on morning visits I get the fidgets and wish I was back home trying to keep up with a hungry newspaper. Each column is a challenge, each takes a long time—and each is read in a few moments and then gone forever.

On this day, a marvelously warm, sunny one, his face was grim.

"You ain't got a screw jack have you?"

Screw jacks aren't that common anymore. Most car jacks are either hydraulic or of the bumper variety. I wondered what kind of load he had to lift.

"I used to have. I may have gotten rid of it. What do you need it for?"

"I got a damn steer stuck in a tree fork."

We went to the little shed, freshly decked out, now, in smoky blue and Navajo red. There I keep all my junk, tools, and oddments. We found the jack, badly rusted, behind a pile of paint cans and tools. The long handle lay with it. "Them hydraulic jacks won't work on their side," Dad said. "Only a screw jack will."

I have had many occasions to appreciate my father's wisdom. Now, after knowing him for forty-eight years, I would have another. He explained that steers scratch on trees and sometimes get their heads down into the forks of the trees and haven't sense enough to raise them. Instead, they fight frantically, sometimes breaking their necks in the process.

The tree was a hackberry, knobby, useless, and the only one on the farm. The steer, a five hundred-pounder, reared and snorted as we approached—and I feared at any moment to hear the dull snap of bones in its neck.

The tree's rough trunk was bright with blood and hair, and the right horn had been knocked off. Dad reached for the steer's nose to try once more and urge its head upward to freedom. But cattle aren't famous for their I.Q.'s.

"Get back!" I yelled, as the animal bellowed and kicked. "He can hurt you bad!"

Placing the jack between the fork, well above the plunging animal, I inserted the long handle and began twisting. Hackberry trees are tough. The jack would not take hold. After several fruitless attempts, Dad got in his truck to go get some steel cable. With it, he would tie to an upper limb and try spreading the tree to free the steer.

I wished I had brought an ax to hack out a purchase point. But even as I thought it, the steer, exhausted by his efforts, sagged to his knees. That meant he would soon choke if he didn't rise, or if the tree were not spread apart. Once more I set the jack and began twisting the handle. "Take hold," I silently urged. "Take hold."

It seemed to be holding. Then I saw the steel tip bite into the tough bark and cranked harder. My arms ached, for they were held high, as the jack itself was set high above the steer. The animal was making choking noises now—yet some instinct caused it to make one last lunge to its feet.

And just like that, it was free.

I stopped cranking. I was sweating, and my arms were paralyzed. The steer loped off, shaking its head. Later, in a chute, Dad would doctor it against screwworms.

The old maroon Dodge appeared over the hill. When Dad arrived, he spotted the jack jammed between the trees. "Got 'er to hold, did you?"

"I got lucky," I said. "But you want to know something, Dad?"
"What?"
"I wouldn't be a farmer for all the tea in Lipton's warehouse."
"Haw, haw, haw!" Dad said.

❧ ❧ ❧

Every so often, between my fifteen-year-old son and me, the subject of How to Live Your Life comes up.

You know how it is if you're a parent. The desire to communicate is well-nigh irresistible. And well it should be, for there are pitfalls on every side which await the unsuspecting. Who can read the future? Certainly not the astrologers, although we have given them every opportunity.

There is the subject of How Long to Stay Out, Care and Maintenance of Autos (coupled with Safe Driving), Matters of the Budget, Respect for Others, and Avoiding Conflicts with the Authorities. I capitalize these few, but there are numerous others that all parents know.

With the stage thus set, father and son edge warily up to the podium for their great debate. Care must be taken here, for personal pride—or sometimes a lack of it—is at stake.

"I think it's time we had a little talk."
"A talk?"
"Yes. And I want you to feel free to jump in at any time. This is not a one-way street, and you have a right to your views."

"Gee, thanks." A dry reply, but at least a reply.

"First off, have you given any thought to your life-style lately?"

"Well . . ." A hesitation. "What do you mean by 'lifestyle'?"

"The way you live your life, of course. You were out *very* late last Saturday night."

"You never told me I had to punch a clock."

"Don't be impertinent! We have rules here, and they have been clearly stated more than once. If I have to constantly worry about where you are, or what you're doing—well, I don't want to complain, but it makes it pretty tough on me."

"Yeah, I guess I see what you mean. I'll get home earlier from now on. Anything else?"

"Well, remember when you backed into that walnut tree?"

"*Me?* I thought that was you!"

"Don't try to weasel out of that by blaming me—*you* did it! Then you drove off, pretending the dent wasn't even there."

A crestfallen look, then, finally, in a low voice: "OK, I admit it—and I'm sorry."

"I trust you'll be more careful in the future. Now—what's this about wanting more of an allowance? We talked about the budget, and agreed there was only so much for Good Times. If you can't live within your budget, there's a career for you in the Congress."

By now, we were both feeling the effects of the first few rounds. Still, we were making progress, and going down the items of transgression step-by-step was a good ploy. There could be no misunderstanding when everything was laid out in the open.

"There is something else, in fact a couple of things. Do you remember last Thursday, when a local farmer's cows came into the yard and polluted the bed of mums growing by the fence?"

"Eh . . . yeah, I guess I do."

"And do you remember cussing both the farmer and the cows?"

A miserable nod of the head established guilt beyond question.

"Well, that shows disrespect for others, and I'm ashamed of you."

"Cripes, his cows showed disrespect for our flowers!"

"Never mind that! The point is, he called the sheriff, and that puts us into conflict with the authorities. The sheriff was very understanding, because he knew that particular farmer had a long history of loose cows. Even so, his job is to act on such complaints—and we could've been fined or taken to court."

We were silent together for a moment. The dreaded task, the confrontation between father and teenage son, was over.

"I hope you understand all this, and that you'll try to do better."

"I will, Son. And thanks."

"You're welcome, Dad."

❧ ❧ ❧

Since time immemorial, the local barbershop has been famed as the place where fishermen gather to swap stories about the biggest fish they ever—or never—caught. The ones that weren't caught would break the most scales.

At such gatherings, enough hot air is expended to inflate a vehicle the size of the Hindenburg.

Mistake me not, I know that fishing has, of late, become a year-round obsession. But catfishing season really doesn't get underway until April, at least down here in the Ozarks. There's a few expeditions before that, but ice-fishing (fishing while covered with ice) isn't that popular in these parts.

On the other hand, barbershop fishing (fishing while enclosed by a warm barbershop) is much practiced. In the abstract, furious battles with giant finsters are handled with superb ease. All that is needed for membership is to have a mouth bigger than the fish that comes out of it.

On one such day, as the barber snipped on a customer, my neighbor Dick popped a piece of spearmint in his mouth and began what we call a "windy."

"It was on the Elk River," he said, crossing his legs and getting comfortable on the bench. "The last flood had washed out a new pool, and an old dead tree had fallen across it. Back in those roots was a perfect place for a lurking catfish. I had driven my Blazer down and, sure enough, when I cast back in there, the water boiled. I felt a whale take my line and I mean a *whale*!

"I knew I was in trouble right off, so I wedged the rod between my bumper and grille and let the rascal tug and pull till he got a bit tired. The minute he slacked off, I wound the line around my winch, started my truck, and got ready to haul that lunker out."

"Well," the barber said, "what happened?"

"He weighed a *ton*," Dick stressed, "so big, he dragged my Blazer a good ten feet before I was able to get him out from under that tree and started winching him in." Pausing for effect, he added: "The heck of it was, before I could get him to shore, an even bigger catfish came up behind and swallered him right down!"

There was a respectful silence for this warm-up effort. Then another angler spoke.

"That ain't nothin' to the time old Tom and I went fishing down at Pudlo's Pond," he said. "Years ago, a *deaf* feller owned that property, but he sold out and went to Texas. That pond covers ten acres and is full of prime catfish and bass."

Pausing a moment, he went on. "Tom and I had been fishin' for half a day, standin' on the bank and talkin' quiet-like. That pond is spring-fed and clear, and we could see them danged fish down ten feet er so! But try as we might, we never got so much as a nibble—and we kept *tellin'* each other what lures t'use and everything!"

For a moody moment he seemed lost in thought. Then he added, "It took a month b'fore Tom and me figured it out: The previous owner had taught them fish lip-reading, and danged if they didn't know everything we said."

This was a good one, as the stony faces showed—for no emotion is betrayed at these sessions.

After a bit, my old fishing buddy Harry spoke up. "Sorta reminds me of the time, oh, four or five years past, when I useta go down on Indian Creek and fish for the really big ones. As you all know, hundred-pound flatheads ain't at all uncommon.

Harry had a reputation for originality, so the bench warmers recrossed their legs and the tempo of the barber's shears picked up.

"Well, I had just got me one of them portable TVs for Christmas. Reckon it was about the size of a small ice-chest, and while I tossed in a mess of chicken-guts on a hook, I watched an old 'Laverne & Shirley' rerun.

"Well, sir, I hadn't been there more'n ten minutes when there was a heck of a swirl o'water, and the biggest catfish I ever saw come up and swallered that TV right down!"

This caused a stir, but the faces remained unperturbed. Finally, the barber said, "And that was the last you ever saw of your TV, eh?"

Harry said, "No sir! Couple of years later, at that same spot, I hooked onto a catfish that must've weighed eighty pounds at least. A couple of buddies helped me get 'im out—and durned if he didn't cough up a TV set right on the spot!"

"That don't prove it was *your* set," the barber pointed out. "Them ol' flatheads'll eat anything. It mighta been somebody else's TV that fish et."

The rest of the fishermen looked at Harry to see how he would get out of this one. Harry smiled coolly and said, "I might agree with you except fer one thing."

"What's that?" the barber asked.

"That TV set was still playin' 'Laverne & Shirley,'" said Harry.

❧ ❧ ❧

Youth seems so far away, and yet it's as near as my inner feelings.

Inside, I am still the twenty-one-year-old kid in the picture on my wall, the one with a row of ribbons on his left tunic and the paratrooper wings above them. There is a glider patch on my overseas cap, cocked at a jaunty angle. My smile is as crisp as new linen, and ah, my friends, and oh, my foes, there is a world yet to be born in those clear eyes.

I was barely out of paratrooper training in that picture. Barely through with screaming corporals mouthing obscenities as they stampeded us into the dawn. Barely through with the hideous first run, three miles in civilian softness, lungs like torches, staggering the last few hundred yards to fall vomiting in the grass.

About half didn't make it and were washed out. For those who made it, there was more of the same. In my group, more little guys made it than big guys. It was harder on the big guys. (When the airborne was first formed in World War II, men over six feet and two hundred pounds were too big. They descended too fast in the old T-7's, and with sixty pounds of equipment on them, they sometimes smashed and broke.)

I still remember those early lectures, sitting in a tin-roofed shed with brains baking, listening to the story of how six men jumped from a Martin bomber in 1928 at Kelly Field, Texas, and set up a machine gun. Our military brass wasn't much impressed with these first paratroopers—but German and Russian observers, invited by the generals, were. By 1936, the Russians had hundreds of training towers and had staged mass military air drops. And in 1941, before our own Eighty-second Airborne was even dreamed of, the Nazis dropped fourteen thousand paratroops on Crete.

How surprised I was to read—for it would never do in 1955 to relate the fact to male trainees—that Kathe Paulus, a woman, made the first jump with a parachute of the type we would use. And she made it, along with many other jumps, in the early days of aviation.

Indeed, a woman first demonstrated the parachute's versatility to the Army. Her name was Tiny Broadwick, and she's also credited with the first free-fall jump and the first deliberate jump into water. World War I had just broken out.

Could the cheerful, grinning eyes in that photograph have ever surmised the path my life would take? There wasn't a hair on my face then, where now there is a forest, but my life's plan was already made. (I had yet to read Robert Burns's poem "To a Mouse" and its famous line, "The best laid plans o' mice and men / Gang aft a-gley.")

My plans called for a military career, but somewhere something went wrong. The drum I started marching to was one nobody else heard. I fell afoul of an officer, went AWOL, and was court-martialed. Gone were my dreams of flying jets. Thanks, lieutenant. You were a lousy leader who never should have been commissioned. But you did me a favor, after all.

Like everyone who was a soldier, I wonder from time to time about the men who crossed my life's path. The buddy who wouldn't jump—he's fifty-three now, if he's around. Jimmy Jones, whose bunk was next to mine and whose parachute failed a week after his wedding. He'd be fifty-three if he were alive.

The bullet-riddled Korean in the muddy ditch. The moon that shone on his upturned face still shines on me. Still shines on the grass in the walnut grove as I step in to gaze at my sleeping son, growing tall and strong, perhaps as some ancient chieftain gazed at his, wondering what the world will do to him—wondering if he'll pass the age I just passed.

The kid in the uniform looks down, forever smiling.

🐾 🐾 🐾

It was one of those slate-gray days when the heavens can't decide whether to blow or rain and the north wind is vigorous enough to make the cattle turn their rumps into it. My folks were on a trip to the West Coast, and I had promised to keep an eye on their farm and livestock.

On this day I trudged across the dead pastures, wrapped up in my fleece-lined coat, wishing that it really were lined with fleece instead of some petroleum-derived plastic fluff.

In this centerpiece of the farm there is a stock pond and a scattering of big oak and walnut trees. But mostly it is pasture, cleared a hundred years ago and once good cropland until it was exhausted. A series of electric poles and crisscrossing barbed-wire fences are the only other obstructions.

As I emerged from a low swale and topped the remains of a 1930s government-built terrace—erected to stem erosion, which, sadly, is still a big threat in Missouri today—I saw a young cow. She stood alone, peculiarly humped even for this cold day. With the herd nowhere near her, she was either sick or calving. As I drew close to her, I saw that it was the latter. From her birth canal protruded the tips of two legs, black-hooved and icy to the touch. Closer examination showed half a head jammed terribly, with a swollen blue tongue clenched between dead teeth.

How long had she stood this way, cramped and hunched in her misery? There was no way to tell. But I knew the calf was dead, and the heifer, a young cow having her first, greatly oversized, calf, would be too—unless I could get a veterinarian to pull the corpse.

I ran the quarter-mile to my trailer and telephoned. By great luck, since veterinarians are almost always on one job or racing to another, I got a young vet at the Neosho Animal Clinic.

"Get her to the barn," he instructed. "She can walk the way she is if you take it slow. I'll get there as soon as I can."

An hour later, he arrived. The heifer was now down, breathing with difficulty as he hooked the chains of his calf-jack around the dead calf's feet. The cow groaned deeply as the vet began cranking, and I feared he would pull her apart. But the oversized calf was slowly coming through the breech—and then suddenly it slid out, plopping in its sodden birth-sack to the floor of the haystrewn stall.

To my surprise, the vet dropped his cranks, grabbed the dead calf, heaved it up onto the flanks of the panting cow, and cleared its mouth of mucus. The corpse rose and fell with the cow's breathing.

"Why are you wasting time with a dead calf?" I asked.

"Take a look," the vet said, grinning—and to my astonishment, I saw the calf begin to breathe. "They're tougher than they look," added the vet, gathering up his tools to leave.

Both cow and calf survived, and that day marked the beginning of my deep respect for D.V.M.'s—veterinarians. Indeed, I respect them as much as I do M.D.'s and believe they must surely know as much— if only because M.D.'s study one type of anatomy while vets must master the puzzling innards of everything from snakes to elephants.

Yet veterinarians, when it comes to status and money, are mostly left wanting. Those in rural areas are about where the old, beloved "country doctor" was fifty years ago. They are on call twenty-four hours a day, every day of the year. Dying animals know nothing of Christmas or Thanksgiving, and many a vet has left a steaming holiday dinner to go and minister to some farmer's sick cow.

Veterinarians perform surgery under conditions that would make physicians throw up their hands and leave, even delivering calves by Caesarean section in snow and mud. And it's the firm belief of most vets that their most difficult cases will occur in the wee hours of a holiday night during a blinding snowstorm.

"You can't just tell a dairyman or swine raiser to take two aspirins and call in the morning," says Rick Wooden, a veterinarian in Anderson. It's hard to understand his grin, because it's an hour past suppertime on a cold, wet day, and he's doing a post-mortem on a calf that has died of pneumonia.

"The worst enemy a vet has is time," he says. "If farmers just call soon enough, there's a much better chance of saving an animal. The longer they wait to see if the condition improves, the more they risk losing a costly animal."

Stockmen don't always see it that way, and to some, not paying the vet has become almost a ritual—regardless of the money vets spend on costly drugs to save a farmer's animal. One pig-raiser in Mc-Donald County has owed a large bill to a veterinarian for months. "Old Ruby just won't pay," he grins. Yet "Old Ruby"—who at eighty is certainly no one's favorite grandmother—recently raced into the Anderson Animal Clinic, grabbed some medicine, and rushed out.

"Wait!" the assistant cried. "You haven't paid for that!"

"I don't *have* to," snorted Ruby. "Ain't got no money—but I need the medicine *anyway*."

"She's probably alienated every vet within fifty miles," says the veterinarians' assistant, Carol Sampson.

The country veterinarians may be the last of the true Samaritans. It takes incredible altruism to rise from a warm bed on a freezing winter night, drive miles to some out-of-the-way Ozark farm, slog through mud or snow to the downed animal—and then risk dangerous infections or injury from flying hooves. And nowhere is all this more beautifully told than in *All Creatures Great and Small,* the autobiography of veterinarian James Herriott, a book I recommend.

I have gone with many country veterinarians on calls. Theirs is a profession that speaks for itself. It is a labor of love—and a love of labor.

✿ ✿ ✿

Sometimes just remembering the shame of things I did as a drunk is enough to make me know I'll finish out my life as dry as a bone. We tend to think of "dry" as desertlike, as devoid of life, as a condition that—in the extreme—is about as attractive as dying of thirst. But the kind of dry I talk about is heaven on earth.

Even as I write, I can think of dozens of friends, people I've known or met casually, and even colleagues who are in the same boat now that I was then. "It can't happen to me," they're saying, as they pour another libation. I've been there. I've said it. I was wrong, and they are, too.

Writers are especially vulnerable to alcohol. History's list of literary lushes is astonishing: Jack Kerouac, John O'Hara, Truman Capote, F. Scott Fitzgerald, Tennessee Williams, Dashiell Hammett, Jack London, Ring Lardner, and the poet Dylan Thomas—who all but disintegrated from booze. And that's just the tip of the ice cube.

A former editor of mine, Frances Ring, chronicles the final months of Fitzgerald. She was his last secretary. Her remembrance, *Against the Current* (Creative Arts Books, Berkeley, California) is a heartbreaking story of a man lost forever to alcohol—who never lived to finish what might have been his greatest book.

Who can count the dreams that have drowned in seas of booze? When we drink, we seem the souls of wit. People hang on our every word, or so we perceive. In truth, they are often regarding us with pity, or disgust, or anger. Booze is the wonderful magic brush that paints the picture as we wish to see it.

Take the time I was visiting friends in Oregon—I won't embarrass them by giving their names—and they took me to an Italian restaurant. The red wine flowed, and soon so did words from my gross and stupid mouth.

I was raucous, belligerent, loud. But I saw myself as clever, superior, forceful. Something I said (good Lord, I don't even remember what) brought tears to the eyes of my host's wife, and I remember thinking, "Why, what's wrong with this silly woman?" I grew angry. She was spoiling a great evening for me.

That was when I became aware of a man standing at my left elbow, a young man with blond hair. In his mid-twenties, he was doubtless one of the thousands of timber workers who thronged that Oregon town.

"Hey, buddy," he said. "Why don't you shut up? I've got my family with me. You're disturbing everybody."

I dimly heard his wife pleading with him to leave me alone. But chances are good that he, too, was feeling his wine, was himself a budding boozer. I'll never know. I stood up, hit him in the jaw, and knocked him down. He was bigger, so I felt a supreme sense of power.

Then he got up—and it was my turn to inspect the wax job, which I did close-up. We brawled all the way outside, where finally a group of men separated us. "The police are coming!" they shouted. Much I cared. I'd take them on, too.

"You ruined a forty-dollar shirt, you S.O.B!" the young man shouted, getting in his car.

"Chicken!" I jeered through my blood.

On the way home, my host was grimly silent and his wife wept.

"The guy was wrong," I said defensively. "He was dead wrong."

"Yeah, sure," my friend said bitterly.

We drove on into the stagnant night.

✿ ✿ ✿

Pete Seeger, the fine folk balladeer, once said that every new-born baby should be given a banjo for his journey through life. I feel that way about porches. Surely it can be said—and ought to be posted on walls—that those who have no porches are lacking one of life's great joys.

Does your city have juvenile delinquency? Is the crime rate too high? Don't send the miscreants to jail. Give them porches. Chain them there if necessary, but give them porches. If their behavior is exceedingly good, allow them a screened porch.

I say this not out of any sympathy for criminals, but out of pity for their lost, porchless years. Had they owned porches, or at least had access to them, they might have grown up straight as a string.

When things went wrong in our family, or when they went right, the porch always played a part. If family pressures became too much, Mom sometimes retired to the front porch and stayed there a while. It helped Dad, too—for, if angered, he liked to be noisy and slam things. A wooden screen door exited the porches of those days, and when he slammed it, the *Bang!* could be heard on the north forty.

In one of the most cunning cures on record, our old family doctor—whose M.D. degree dated to horse-and-buggy days—was called in as a consultant for a child who was slowly wasting away. The boy's parents were very wealthy, and had called specialists in from New York, St. Louis, and Denver. None of their elixirs or potions did a thing, though, and the poor little tyke, propped on velvet and silk by a great picture window, grew worse. His parents were distraught. They turned to Doc in despair, and he did not let them down.

"Build that boy a porch and put him on it," he said firmly—and left all those other fancy doctors with their jaws hanging open.

The father did so without delay, and soon the lad was laughing and playing with his friends as if he'd never been sick at all.

To date, no porches have been reported to cure cancer, but the news could come at any time.

Porches and how to build them have obviously been deleted from all architectural studies in favor of something called a deck. I have known for years what a deck was. It belongs on a ship, and used to stay there. Then apparently some ex-sailor became the dean of a college of carpentry and decided to make his mark at the expense of the rest of us.

As near as I can tell, most city builders (and this overflows like a mudslide into small towns) deck their various halls. These dinky "porchlets" are usually big enough to allow a couple of adults to stand side-by-side and gaze at the wall next door. But it's easy to see why they are named nautically—they are about the size of a crow's nest on a schooner.

The waste of a mind is a terrible thing, and somewhere out there some wonderfully creative ones—minds that dream of porches and might build some—are being wasted. But we get what we deserve. If porches allow our imagination to roam amid fireflies and thunderheads and hear a distraught violin in a mosquito's song, well, decks make our arches hurt and give us migraines.

Rip out the damnable decks I say! Threaten your builder until he agrees to erect a good, sturdy, old-fashioned, spacious porch! Rush forth to congratulate those pioneers who, having found porches intact on grand but tottery old homes, restored them complete with screens!

St. Louis was once a city of porches. Would you have it be known as the city of little decks?

※ ※ ※

I have seen it coming for years, and worried about it. But I knew there was little I could do. Advancing age is a fact of life, and it comes for all of us.

Some people can whistle through it—and sometimes he does. Others whine, or complain, or simply lie around in a state of lethargy that brings despair to those of us who must cope with it.

Now, it has become worse. There is the absent-mindedness, becoming more alarming the older he gets. Sometimes he forgets who he is, and if introduced to strangers murmurs "Uh . . . Uhh" and seems helpless to continue. In social situations he is lost in a world of his own, and not much will bring him out of it. Lord knows, I love him—but it does get wearying.

His lack of coordination is another cause for concern. Not long ago, driving the pickup in the pasture at night, he went to back up and turned too sharply. The right front fender collided with a tree. He wasn't hurt, thank goodness, but the insurance wouldn't cover it. A good local body man, Garland Walters, did a patch-up for $125, and I paid for it.

"You shouldn't be driving at night," I scolded. He made no excuse.

He doesn't make excuses, I'll give him that. And he still has a sense of duty and responsibility—even if he's not always able to carry them out as he might like. Except for the slow stack-up of days that seems to make of him something different than he ever was before, being with him is a pleasure. I wish I could manage to spend more time with him, but he understands the pressures of this busy life.

I kid him about his clumsiness, which he accepts with good nature. Sometimes he gives as good as he gets—and I find out what it's like to be on the receiving end. A sense of humor is easy to have when the barbs are turned on someone else. It's not so easy when they're aimed at you.

Many times I've tried to interest him in more social activities, but he seems content without them. True, we live six and a half miles from the nearest town—but so do many folks. It's even a struggle to get him away from the TV set.

And I can't count the times when his hearing has seemed impaired. I've had to yell more than once, upon walking into the house and finding the sink piled high with dirty dishes.

"Good grief! Don't you ever wash a dish?"

"Don't you ever stop complaining?" I can hear him thinking—and sometimes he gives me a look of both resignation and exasperation. At times like that, I try to ease up, for I know this whole aging business is hard on both of us. (They call my generation the Sandwich Generation because we are caught between the old and the young. But today, the pendulum is swinging more towards the old. We're becoming a geriatric nation.)

So the seasons pass for each of us, and that's how it should be. What we can't help, we ought not to hinder. He's moving on up the ladder of years and so am I. There'll never cease to be periods of adjustment.

He sleeps a lot and is harder to wake up than a stump. He's most active when he's with the dogs, for they leap and cavort around him.

Sometimes he surprises me and even summons energy for a brisk run with them.

Maybe I shouldn't be so concerned.

Jason is pretty normal for a fifteen-year-old.

✿ ✿ ✿

Those who have never tasted homemade sorghum should not confuse it with the strong, dark molasses carried by supermarkets. Amber in color, sorghum is as gentle on the tongue as nectar, and carries with it all the fragrance of a summer's day. You can't buy homemade sorghum unless you know something about the maker that he doesn't want known. Then you might be able to blackmail him out of, oh, say a teaspoonful—but even then you'd have to put his toes in a vise and crank the handles. "It's the sweetest taste this side of heaven," sorghum-lovers vow.

In 1983, I traveled to Tuscumbia, Missouri, to check out a rare source of ever-dwindling sorghum-making. Half a mile short of the Osage River, I turned into the drive of a neat white-frame house. Atop a knoll, near a small shed, several pickup trucks were parked. It was a cloudy day with some nippiness in the air—but men were in shirtsleeves. The work of making sorghum, and the fire in the huge firepan, conspire to make them perspire.

I was met by a remarkably spruce gentleman, Clyde Hawken, who is almost eighty but moves with the crispness of a man of fifty. "I see you found us," he said. "Wasn't sure if Lucy gave you the right instructions." Lucy, Hawken's wife, was at a club meeting. But this is pretty much "man's work," and the old ethic prevails: Women make the harvest dinner, men do the sorghum-making.

Clyde showed me around, explaining as we walked. "We bring the cane in from the field and stack it just so . . ." He pointed to several evenly piled hillocks of cane. "Then it's taken to the crusher, where one of us feeds it through the rollers."

The sorghum mill bore the legend "Mohawk 8, L.M. Ramsey Mfg. Co., St. Louis, Missouri, 1882."

"A hundred and one years old!" I exclaimed, and Clyde smiled.

"There's a few still around that's even older," he said, "but they're gettin' almost impossible to find, and no one is making them any-more." He showed where the old walking-pole shaft had been cut off. "This one has been modified so we can hook a belt to it and run it by a tractor's power take-off."

A blue-and-white Ford 2000 tractor with a wide belt stretching like an umbilical cord quietly purred. Then a man advanced the throttle, engaged the clutch—and the crew of six men were back at work.

Hawken's crew consisted of his brother Carl, sixty-nine; Jay Wallace, seventy-five; Virgil Burks, sixty-six; Robert Annett, forty-seven; and Floyd Johnson, sixty-eight. Annett, a burly, dark-haired man with a steady smile—the youngest man there—may be the salvation of this annual custom. Johnson, the only active farmer, and Clyde Hawken are teaching him all they know. "Like as not," Hawken said, "this'll be our last year for sorghum squeezin'. But I think Bob'll keep on doin' it."

Sorghum (also known as milo) is cut between September 15 and October 15, with some variance. In any case it must be harvested before frost, or it will be ruined. Cutting the stuff is hard, fast, itchy work, and once cut it must be processed as speedily as possible to avoid flavor changes. Once run through the crusher, the juice flows down a trough to a bucket. This is emptied into an oak barrel equipped with a spigot and mounted at the elevated end of the long rectangular trough where the juice is cooked.

The pan is about twelve feet long and holds around a hundred gallons of squeezin's. It must be mounted on a special bed of clay, which spreads the heat evenly. The whole is mounted on sledlike runners, although in the past sorghum mills were often stationary—like cotton gins—and farmers brought their sorghum to the miller, who took a portion of the syrup as payment.

The fire under the cooking pan is fed by seasoned oak, usually old fallen trees or fence posts. "They make the hottest, most evenly burning fire," according to Bob Annett.

One other modern touch lies with the portable propane tank and nozzle that can be held by one man, with a jet of gas shot into the furnace when faster heat is desired.

Vigorous boiling, like a series of tiny eruptions, resembles cat feet—and is the signal that the heat is just right. Meanwhile, the boiling liquid must be constantly skimmed with a device resembling an old woodstove ashes-scoop. This cigar-box shape, handmade of metal, removes the green scum that rises during the cooking process. This is tossed into a nearby "gosh hole."

"Why the name?" I asked.

"Step in that slop and you'll know why," chuckled T. A. Clark, seventy-six, a retired carpenter who had arrived to help. As a boy, Clark moved sorghum mills all over the country—wherever one was needed.

"Dad had his own mill," he recalled, "and we planted sorghum as a cash crop back during World War I."

Floyd Johnson was busy filling jugs and big lard cans with cooked sorghum syrup. The fragrance surrounding the site was heavenly, somewhat similar to orange-blossom perfume. Johnson brought a quart jar of the syrup and gave it to me. "Try that on some hot biscuits with lots of butter," he said. "Then you write and let me know if you've ever had anything as good."

It was more than a generous gesture, because I know the gift came out of his portion. All the sorghum from the squeezin' is always spoken for, often many months before the crop is even harvested.

The making of sorghum syrup is an art that desperately needs to be passed on—but apparently the hard work involved scares away the young folks today who might otherwise help preserve this vanishing bit of Americana.

Several of the remaining few sorghum makers have quit making it in the past few years. My search only turned up two makers. Clyde Hawken, and a gentleman in Arkansas who refused to be written about. It seems he was caught by revenue agents, disguising the smell of a moonshine still with the fragrant fumes from a sorghum mill.

The flavor of freshly made sorghum lies somewhere between the taste of ambrosia and the delights of nectar—food, some say, that is fed to the angels. If it's good enough for them, it's good enough for me. So all that's left to say is: "Dear Floyd Johnson—Thanks for the sorghum. It was all you claimed and more. I still have about a pint left, into which I sometimes dip a toothpick so it will last longer. The only trouble is, it's a bit inconvenient to get to, locked as it is in my safety deposit box."

138

※ ※ ※

Ozark mists are like no others. They can shift, move, turn as the sun rises behind them, making swirling patterns that gradually lighten and finally disappear. Or you can top a rise and be in cold, clear glittering night, with stars cutting holes in the black sky above you while down in a swale or holler a white band of fog chalks out the middle of trees, so the tops float like anchorless blimps. Just recently, I rolled out of bed at 5:30 A.M. to let the cat out of the house—and discovered a perfect Ozark mist.

On a morning like that one promised to be, bed was out of the picture. By the time I'd showered and had my low-calorie breakfast of coffee in hot skim milk with brown sugar, dawn was a presence instead of a promise.

In minutes, overalled and straw-hatted, I saddled my shanks' mare and was off at a lope. There was just enough frost on the pasture grass to make the earth springy under my feet, and although at my age I'm rebuilding the temple with caution, I couldn't help breaking into a run every few yards.

The air was so thick and rich with oxygen it was like having new lungs—and my own Olympic gold now hung above the trees, softly shrouded by fog. Through the heavy mists wavering around me, the sun looked like the headlamp of an old-time freight train spinning through the dimness, haloed by expanding circles of light.

On the middle hill of Dad's three-hilled pasture, I stopped by the knotted hugeness of a stump. Big as a car, it bulged from the earth—all that remained of a limbless, lightning-shattered oak that once lifted its trunk forty feet into the air. What a landmark it made, twisting upward from its bulbous base like a giant onion. When Dad chainsawed it ("It coulda fell an' hurt m' cows!"), we almost went to fist city.

Now something made me turn. And there, perched above the lavender mists like a china plate, a full moon shone. It was such a striking contradiction—glaring moon and soft sun facing each other—I nearly shouted for joy. I've been in some of Europe's grandest cathedrals, but they were made by man—and this was made by nature.

Words from an old song drifted like mist through my mind, the kind of song that mingled joy and sadness, that had no grotesque faces cavorting or laser lights knifing through marijuana smoke . . . the kind of world that isn't around anymore.

"In the sky the bright stars glittered / On the shore the pale moon shone / It was from Aunt Dinah's quilting party / I was seeing Nelly home."

"Bwawww!"

A little foghorn had gotten lost from its mother, part of the crop of calves that had begun to appear in the pastures. Instantly, a concerned "Bwoom! Bwoom!" came from the thinning patches, and here came mama at a run. Or at a float. All around me now, cows were looming out of the mist like suspended melons, their legs cut off by lowering bands of fog.

Ahead, the trees bordering Dad's eastern pasture were so fog-shrouded they looked like Civil War women in ballooning gowns—Tara's society ball served up in silver.

At the corner of the fence line, near the big oak by the black tire that holds herd salt, I cranked right. Half a mile down that fence was the old farmhouse Dad mostly lets get older, though once he had given it a new roof.

The moon still sailed serenely along, to my right now, and the violet mist was holding. But the rising sun was paling the trees to amber, and dawn had become daylight.

The morning was made doubly fine because my mom was in a rare tranquil mood—and I found myself loving her again, as I had loved her when she was young and sang a lot, and not sick, as she's become in her old age. Mom has been ill for a very long time.

To her, the fog is a sad and miserable thing. No sunrises bring her joy. Nothing brings her joy. And Dad, who has loved her through many years and many leavings, patiently accepts her endless tirades about the life she wasted "havin' kids and hoein' cotton."

But it's never Mom talking, not really. It's a mist, swirling through her mind, one she fears and fights, one that could someday consume her completely.

Or perhaps someday there will be sunlight breaking through.

❀ ❀ ❀

I was working under the walnut trees one recent sunny day when a sound caught my attention—a soft, sighing whisper, rising from pure silence into something like a moan. I knew what it was—the last breath of autumn.

The wind picked up, rustled the few leaves left in the walnut grove, plucked the remaining walnuts and dropped them with a thunk-thunk all around me, and finally descended on the patch of oaks, hickories, and mulberries sloping northward from my trailer.

I turned to see a gentle shower of gold raining down in the woods, hundreds of leaves leaving this life behind, as silent in their final going as they had been in their arrival a year ago. Even after the wind had died, not a breeze passing through the ranks of trees, the leaves still sifted down like molten snowflakes, rocking belly first or slowly spiraling toward their last duty—the creation of new soil as their bodies rot under countless spring rains.

It is a sight I never weary of, something to brighten even the grayest of days.

We humans take such pride in our short lives, appointing a luster to ourselves that often we wear ill. We give ourselves souls, yet deny the privilege to anything else. There are some religions, of course, that see an animus in things that aren't animal—and what's the harm of that? Is the mission of a leaf any less important than the mission of a human?

I think about these tiny questions, having pondered all the weighty human ones until my head aches, twice a year: In the spring, when new leaves curl toward life like little green tongues, and in the fall, when winter starts raking them into windrowed piles with its hard breezes.

As I came up the dirt road that leads to my place late one morning, the south-slanting sun was exactly right to catch the turning leaves and illuminate them. Despite a dry summer, it was a spectacular fall in most of the Ozarks, especially in this corner of Missouri, Arkansas, and Oklahoma. A killing frost had turned the road into a technicolor tunnel of reds, golds, bronzes, and purples. The light from the sun turned each leaf into a tiny bulb. Ribs and veins stood out,

and stray breezes gave the leaves a strange, shivery life all their own—
a life that ended almost as soon as it had begun.

Earlier, I had visited the home place to talk with Dad and help him
and the vet vaccinate some cattle. Frost stood like icing on my truck's
windshield, and the thermometer held at thirty. In Dad's garden,
green pepper plants were wilted, their leaves hanging down like the
wet hair of a maiden fresh from a river. Giant pods of okra, long since
too tough to eat, hung on stripped stalks like forlorn fingers.

The final days of fall affect animals differently than they do humans. Humans become pensive, drawing into themselves in dread of
the four frozen months to come. Animals—especially dogs—frisk
and leap, sniffling the earth with eager noses. Yearling calves race
across pastures green from recent rains. The hay is in the barn, the
trees almost bare. The time of yearly reckoning is at hand.

"I reckon I'll get rid o' them chickens in the spring," says Dad.
"They ain't layin' any eggs."

"Reckon we could go visit my brother over in Heavener?"
asks Mom.

It's a time of tucking in, of repairing the heated water trough so it
won't freeze and keep the cows from drinking. Those cows, as the
whole family knows, are Dad's main reason for living. They are his
pets, and every year the winnowing process gets more difficult
for him—for it's hard to send an old cow, however worthless, to the
sale barn.

For me, looking at the barren woods, the dark trunks stripped and
ready for swirling snow, it's a time to reflect on how swiftly this year
has passed—and how my life is one year shorter. At fifty-one, I can
no longer deny my mortality as I could at forty-one, or laugh in the
face of time as I did at twenty-one.

As I said good-bye to the folks and got in my pickup to return
home, the lines from an old verse ran through my mind—part of a
nineteenth-century poem by a woman who tried to make winter a
joyful time. Mom used to recite it as we gleaned the last few bolls
from after-frost cotton, and it has stayed with me for almost forty
years.

Come little leaves,
Said the wind one day,

Across the meadows
With me to play,
Put on your dresses
Of red and gold,
The days grow short,
And the wind grows cold. . . .

✿ ✿ ✿

---

hey had been married almost forty-six years—years of hard
work that included raising their four children, for the family worked as cottonpickers for much of their life together.
The man was sixty-eight, and the woman was seventy. Overweight
and in bad health, she was loading her car when I drove up.

"I'm leaving him," she announced. "I've lived with that man as
long as I can stand it."

She brushed a hand through hair the color of iron filings. Once it
had been Irish red and naturally wavy.

"I got me a place in town," she explained. "I'm takin' my half of
the Social Security."

The husband would stay on their seventy-acre farm, caring for the
cattle. "It's all he's ever done," she said bitterly. "He thinks more of
them cows than he ever did of me or his kids."

Some neighbors come to help, and while she takes a load to her
apartment we talk. One thinks she is making things too easy for the
husband. Others point out that he has been very patient with her
behavior, seldom responding to her almost constant tirades. Some
nights he sleeps in his pickup in the pasture.

But I know that both people have their good sides, too. They
raised four children through some hard times. And if they seldom
openly displayed love, both have physically saved their kids' lives. The
mother once dragged them from a burning shack. The father smashed
his only shotgun over the face of a bull charging his son.

I know, too, that once they were in love. They met in Mesa, Arizona, in 1936 and were married a year later. She already had a son,
whose own father had disappeared before the child's birth. He was a
hand-milker at a dairy, a hard but steady job. Soon a daughter was

born, then a son, a "blue baby" who almost died, and finally another daughter. Then the milking job came to an end.

In the waning days of the Depression the whole family picked cotton under the broiling sun of California, Arizona, Texas.

In 1941, the husband worked as a copper miner. Then he moved his family to Oklahoma and began sharecropping.

Most of the time, there was no crop to share. The family knew extreme poverty, and at time there was barely enough food to eat—usually just "blue john" gravy over biscuits or a pot of beans seasoned with cheap cuts of salt pork.

The husband began a life-long love affair with used cars, buying them over his wife's objections, plunging the family deeper in debt. She once said bitterly that he'd had "one car for every year we been married," and she was right.

They quarreled constantly, often awakening the kids with their shouts and screams. But the kids learned how to be rubber bands. If they fathomed anything, it was not the neurotic behavior of their parents. Even the whippings the kids got didn't trouble them for long. But they resented the ragtag clothes they wore to school—when they got to go to school. And they envied the soft white bread other kids took for lunch. They packed biscuits smeared with margarine.

Their parents' quarrels became physical. Once they saw their father bloody their mother's nose. She retaliated by hurling a brass alarm clock and laying his forehead open. Blue-coated police officers came, and their parents spent the night in jail while the kids stayed with a neighbor.

There were good, peaceful times too. Moments when the family picnicked by a grassy canal. Times when father and sons fished in a chablis-colored California brook. But these hours were few.

For the most part the kids grew up OK. But today two of them have serious drinking problems, and one has had five husbands.

In 1951, the oldest son escaped to the Korean War, so the father, lacking a helper, gave up sharecropping and moved back to California, where he became a plumber. The kids began leaving home as quickly as they could, for the bickering and the fights continued as before. Then one day in 1967 the father took all the money he could from his bankrupt plumbing business and vanished.

At loose ends for a while, his wife finally went to Iowa where the oldest son was in graduate college. Neither of them knew the husband was working on construction in the same city using an assumed name. One day an astonished son ran into him in a bar.

Then in their late fifties, husband and wife patched things up once more. In a last grab for the brass ring, they bought a Missouri farm. By 1982 they were comfortable, and the farm was paid for. But she would not let him forget his past mistakes. And her temper had gotten worse, not better.

So, Mom and Dad, you've finally come to the end of a long, hard row. That's what we used to say in our cottonpicking days, when we had worked to exhaustion—as you have in your marriage. Perhaps it's to your credit that you tried longer than most to make the best of a bad situation.

I love you, and so do your other kids. The debt we owe you far exceeds our abilities to ever repay it.

It's too bad that the passing years could not ease your anger and your anguish. It hurts to know that in the funeral of your life together, we can only bow our head and stand aside, and hope that somehow you find happiness.

4

Winter comes with all a winter's promise,
and still the flowers bloom by my front door.
I dropped their seeds as late as late September,
and now they face December with a calmness
denied by their stiff stance against my wall.
I ask if they feel pain when, winter tossed,
their rigid leaves are tentacled by frost,
or what they feel, or if they feel at all.
My flowers give no warmth and ask for none:
each petal surrounds its own consistent sun
in perfect symmetry. I have known worse
arrangements that were called a universe.

There is a time in the Ozarks when fall and winter balance on the same breaking hinge—when the gate of seasons creaks rustily to and fro, as if undecided about which way to go.

Those are showcase days. Autumn, paying its final court to an earth that will soon be frozen and white, flings colors like a painter gone mad. And winter, aware of its power, plays along with silver-and-gold settings of sunrises and frosts.

One misty morning before winter overtook us, I headed down the pasture hill, east towards the dark line of Dad's woods, and past the huge, knobby stump of the oak tree killed by lightning—and finally felled by Dad's saw.

I make little noise when I walk, but they still heard me and were gone in a whistle of wings. Five mallard ducks had been floating on Dad's pond. Now they were airborne, adrift in the sky like beads burst from a string. I tracked them with upraised arms and pointing fingers, but I hadn't been duck-hunting since the game warden's son took me down along Buffalo Creek four years ago—and even then I hunted with a camera. *Brrrr!* Duck-hunters must have antifreeze in their veins.

Everywhere I saw the signs of winter. It was saying, "No more Mister Nice Guy," and even though we'd had only one snap frost to aluminize the grass and fallen leaves, the real thing lay just ahead.

While we waited for the thermometer to plummet, there were rewards. Six days of rain and drizzle finally gave way to a single day of sun so bright, it was like living among mirrors. Each livestock pond, every wet leaf, even the hard field stones shone with jewel-like luster. The wind, soon to be allied with winter's bitter cold, was not yet ready to stop its fall frolics—and no sooner had the sun dried the leaves than the wind began to toss them into the air like confetti.

Coming up the steep grade from Pole Cat Holler, I saw a glittering cloud of gold spangles rise in front of me—a whirlwind had lifted the fruits of someone's labor high into the air. For awhile it snowed gold, and then I left the leaves behind to head on home with my groceries.

On that morning, Dad was as cranky as a freshly unhibernated bear. I've been tape-recording as many of his memories as he will part with, because some day (that favorite phrase of writers) I hope to weave them into a book.

But that day, I soon shut the recorder off, for he was tired of the unceasing rain, the endless parade of grayness, and was cussing with considerable energy. "This is the tee-total-*damnedest* weather I have ever seen" was one of his milder outbursts. "Ain't it ever gonna clear up?"

"Better get used to it," I said. "There's plenty more ahead."

He had already forgotten how hard the humid summer had made it for him to breathe.

Later that day, as afternoon passed into late afternoon, the gray sky began paling and diluting into blue. By sundown, only a single pearly mass of clouds graced the western horizon—and as I watched from my study window, an apple-red sun slid out from under them.

For a moment, it was a scene of sheerest beauty, like being inside the lustrous confines of a great, pink shell, with the cloud being the flesh, and the sun some incredible new kind of seaborn pearl—a scarlet pearl that nestled there in the chamber of the sky.

And then it was gone.

❄❄❄

The warm weather was holding as I stepped outside my trailer one early winter night to smell the air and marvel at the stars. They were worth marveling at. It was as if some jeweler had flung handfuls of silver sand on an obsidian beach.

The trees—tall, slender walnuts and thick-boled oaks—were bathed in reflected light. But not from the stars. Almost hidden by twigs and branches, the yard light installed by the power company leaked light in splayed patterns from high on a pole.

Near the northwest end of my trailer stands a walnut tree that is a gauge of my life. When I came here it was the smallest, most spindly tree in the grove, standing perhaps fifteen feet high. By contrast, its neighboring twenty-five- and thirty-footers were giants. Now the "runt" is a hefty tree thirty-five feet tall, while all its sylvan kin have reached towering heights indeed.

The tree reminds me of someone who has now been a part of my life all those years. He and his family have been neighbors, confidants, helpers, and workers. I have seen his children grow from little shavers to teenagers and young ladies, had them trick-or-treat me, heard of their illnesses, listened to their shouts ringing like fine crystal on the winter air.

It's hard to describe the Shavers, even though I've known them longer than I've known any neighbors. They are a freedom-loving family, good workers, and poor. Yet saying they are poor, even in material things, isn't quite the case. Because Kenny Shaver can skin most anybody when it comes to trading.

It's how he's cushioned the raw edges of living for his family over the years. A skilled cabinet-maker who has mastered a variety of other skills, Kenny is proudest of his "horse trading" ability. When times were harder than just hard, or when he couldn't find jobs or chores to do, Kenny would scour the piles of junk in his yard or scattered among his oak grove and come up with something to trade.

For quite a while after my arrival, I was one of his willing customers. He would come over with some piece of junk or other and by a sorcery known only to him make the rusted or broken artifact seem rarer than the Star of India. Nor would he lie to make the gadget—or garbage—seem better than it was.

"Now Chilly, I wouldn't want ye t'think this here ol' motor uz any good. It's been a-layin' out there in th' trees, an'. . ."

"I understand. Let me have it."

"Ennyways, I ain't sure I'd sleep good, knowin' I sold ye a motor that warn't no good . . ."

"I know. Let me have it. It's just what I need."

"I ain't a-sayin' it *won't* run, mind ye—I'm jist a-sayin' it *mightn't* run. . ."

"That's fine, just fine. I like to tinker. Here's $100."

". . . on accounta it *ain't* run fer nigh onto five years." A long pause, during which Kenny would study the clouds, the limbs of trees, the flight of birds—while I pressed money into his hand.

"Now, Chilly, dang it, that's jist th' trouble—ye're too dang generous fer yer own good! Now that there motor ain't worth *half* what yer a-tryin' t'pay me fer it." Kenny ends such an absolution by pocketing—reluctantly—whatever I have offered.

It is not a one-way exchange. I am still under his spell. Even if that motor, or whatever I have bought, is nothing but rust from one end to the other, I am proud—no, *honored* to have it. And that is the secret of Kenny Shaver's success as a trader. He makes you glad you've been skinned. He could make a bobcat delighted with that same treatment, performed without anesthesia. You have to admire talent like that.

Over the years, this lanky, chain-smoking, slow-talking hill dweller has swapped me out of some decent items. But I've always been convinced that he's more than evened-out the horse-trading, and I've always considered it my good fortune to know him, his petite and quiet wife, and their quartet of kids.

The Shavers are the best of mountain people, although outsiders with limited powers of observation, or with biases bigger than their intelligence, might wonder at such a description. Kenny and his family put on no airs, accept no counsel, and in the parlance of rural folks, plow their own rows. Yet I have never had a problem that I couldn't ask Kenny's help with—whether it's a pipe burst by a winter freeze or trouble installing a new bathroom. He's done more to keep my old trailer together than anyone else around.

Best of all, he's a good neighbor. He really cares about those he likes—and if I need his help with anything, I have only to call him. At the same time, he wouldn't stop to spit on those he doesn't like. To him, life is a marketplace that can have either friends or enemies.

Kenny drifts along in his world as all of us do in ours. He'll skin a friend in a trade as quick as he'll skin an enemy.

The difference is, he only helps his friends.

✳ ✳ ✳

Blue sky, white sun, and rolling green hills. A rare early-winter day in southwestern Missouri—where you would think weather would be warmer than it really is. (Sometimes the wind chill can sink temperatures to twenty below zero and more, although it is always warmer at the lower elevations.)

Dad had recently had a heart bypass, so I walked to his place to feed his cows for him. After grunting the bales of hay into the pickup, I headed out across the lowest of three pastures. Dad has made those critters his pets—and they crowded around the tailgate, jostling me as they tried to yank off hunks of hay.

"Hee-aah, *he-ahh!*"

A lion would cower at my roaring, but cows are dumb, dumb, dumb. That's why they have such a peaceful look on their faces. When Ma Nature said "brains," they thought she said "grains"—and looked around for a creep-feeder. Rather than get crushed against the truck, I took off my heavy leather belt and began laying about me. The tactic brought me enough room so I could toss several slabs of hay back over their heads—which most of them went after.

Strangely, I was reminded of a time in Bombay when I stepped out of the Intercontinental Hotel into a sea of crying, jostling humanity—all of them beseeching me for rupees. I was a guest of India, there to write tourism stories for magazines. The phalanx facing me and two other writers consisted of beggars, professional and otherwise.

Then I caught sight of a little girl. She couldn't have been more than eleven—a thin stalk with huge, starved eyes and a face pinched with hunger. But that wasn't all. One of her bare feet was horribly awry, twisted so that the toes faced rearward. It had been bound that way by the beggar chief who had purchased her as a baby. I looked around. Was that kind-faced old man with white hair, a bowl in his hand, his dark eyes hidden—was he a monster in disguise?

There was no way of knowing. The mob was pressing closer, crying out for money. My companions suddenly took handfuls of change and threw them toward the rear—and the beggars melted away. All except the child with the twisted foot. I put the money in my hand into her own matchstick fingers. Before long, it would be in the hands of the man who owned her body—and had long since robbed her soul. I couldn't help but think of my own children back home.

I drove the pickup back to the barn where Dad's Limosin bull, a runty fellow who nonetheless throws fine calves, was waiting for his ration of grain.

He's the only animal Dad wants grained, for he is somewhat run-down after a strenuous summer of obeying requests from cows. He hasn't much choice in the matter. Come to think of it, the cows don't either. Hormones start humming, instincts are aroused, and nine months from that moment Dad will be out counting a new calf crop.

There was a five-gallon plastic bucket by the granary door, and I dumped several scoops of feed into it. A mixture of cracked corn, wheat, milo, minerals, and molasses, the stuff smelled delicious. Once, beguiled by the aroma as a youth, I had taken a mouthful. Frankly, I don't see what cattle see in it. It has about as much flavor as mud—which I'd also taken a mouthful of once.

For reasons best known to him, Buster (Dad names all his cattle) regarded me with something that wasn't affection. I guess he sensed that I'd had enough of his kind as a boy on the farm. Maybe he fathomed, deep in his curly dome, that I had not worked my way through seven years of college to end as his servant. Regardless, Buster walked sedately through the narrow wooden gate. I followed with the bucket held low, and . . . *wham!*

Some people think only horses and mules can kick backward, but they are misinformed. Buster's hindquarters had gauged the distance from them to me, and two thick hooves landed with a loud *crack!* And I, who had never been an admirer of plastic, found myself appreciating the mangled bucket with spilled contents that lay in the mud at my feet: My shins stung from abrasions, but most of the bull's force was absorbed by the bucket. I backed out of the corral. Buster looked at me. I glared at him.

"If you weren't such a runt," I gritted, "I'd thrash you within an inch of your life."

Actually I said something a lot different, but Buster didn't care in any case. He was snuffling at the spilled grain. Buster, and all bulls, are reminders that farm animals can hurt you, even kill you. No matter how placid they look, they're rarely pets—and Ozark visitors must know this.

As a local farmer put it on a big sign: "If You Can't Cross My Pasture In 9.5 Seconds, Stay Out. My Bull Can Do It In 9.6."

✻ ✻ ✻

I t was such a perfect day for death it might have been written in a book. But winter was the author of the story that unfolded before me, a story that had its beginnings far back in the mists of ages—and ended here in the mists of a rocky hill-farm.

Even the clouds cooperated, lumbering low and darkly gray across the Ozarks as I headed home from Dad's after haying his cows. I saw the rainbow sparks of Christmas lights half a mile away, ringing the trailer like many-hued fireflies. The lights usually eased the winter gloom—but the walnut trees were twigged and stark under the caul of the sky.

"Y'll find 'im off the fence row a bit," Dad had said. "Layin' about thirty yards out. Ain't no bigger'n a dog."

"Was he born alive?"

"Naw, and it's just as well he wasn't. I cain't use no runts."

I threw the last of the bales onto Dad's four-wheel-drive pickup, and we headed out into a pasture made swampy by recent rains. So far Dad's recovery from a fiveway heart bypass had only been so-so, and his chest muscles still had not regained the strength necessary to hoist forty-pound hay bales over his head for stacking.

"Any idea why the calf was born dead?" I asked as he drove, and Dad shook his head.

"It coulda been any number o' things. She's been in poor condition all year. That mighta caused it—I'll just have t'call the vet and find out."

The death of an animal for any reason is cause for concern to the small farmer. Dad and Mom were back together, at least temporarily, and they depended on Dad's herd to supplement their Social Security by bringing in a few dollars more at cattle auctions. Even a new calf born dead meant the eventual loss of several hundred dollars— the price of the calf as a yearling.

I broke and scattered the hay bales and headed home. The dead calf was in the center pasture, Dad said, and I walked down the east-west fence, looking for it. I found it lying in the center of a birth-circle. Grass and mud from the mother's hooves told of her labors to expel what had become a foreign object that—if left unborn—could eventually kill her.

The tiny form lay on its back, oddly vulnerable to the gritty sleet that had begun to fall. The rear legs were splayed, but the forelegs lay together on the left side of the body in a bovine imitation of prayer. The bull calf was scarcely bigger than a small dog, and what would have become hair was only pale yellow peach-fuzz. Spring is the normal time for calving. It was midwinter, so the calf was no more than half-term.

How finely formed it was, bearing in its tiny body all the bones and blood vessels it would have carried through its life. How many million years of nature's trials and errors had brought it to this final shape and destiny. Or perhaps some other miracle imprinted signals in its genes, messages that foretold its death before its life had scarcely begun.

I knelt by the frozen form, feeling a strange kinship with the little animal nature had said no to. How lightly most of us take life, never dreaming how quickly it is gone. And who is the better off, those who never start at all—or those who finish the journey and sometimes find it a bitter one?

But everything has a purpose in the Ozarks. This death would mean life for wild animals that found the calf. And the mother's abortion at nature's command had saved her life as well.

I rose, taking a last look at the body that would be gone by this time tomorrow. What was done was done. It was time to get on with other things. Glancing up at the sky, I saw that it was growing lighter. Perhaps the sun would break through.

❀❀❀

The back door of the trailer was frozen shut, and I had to kick the bottom to break the glazed ice that had frozen in the cracks and hinges. The minute it opened, I wished I had left it closed. A north wind so cold the air seemed like blue electricity struck and numbed my face in seconds.

I had seen the thermometer earlier—zero degrees Fahrenheit. But it was on the porch, out of the wind. This was my first experience with a truly glacial wind, which surely brought the chill-level to at least thirty below zero. For a moment I felt like ice-age man, peering from a hole in a hillside, seeking signs of life in a frozen wasteland. "Oh, joy," I said—for Dad's forty cows had to be fed.

Dad's recovery had not gone well. Originally, the feeling was that he would be good as new three to six months after bypass surgery— and back doing light work in six weeks. And so he was. But in the eighth postoperative week, after telling me he could tumble bales off the truck if I loaded them the night before, he started becoming short of breath again. Then he flunked his stress test on the medical treadmill—and we were back to square one.

I knew this was a terrible blow to Dad. He had pinned his hopes on being able to maintain his farm until he was eighty—whereas I and all his kids wished he would sell the place and move into town. But the other kids were all on the West Coast, while I—the oldest at fifty-two—lived within a mile. So when Dad became ill and opted for heart surgery, I was it. My life would have to be adjusted to where I could help him over the hump, as it had been during his crisis with the brown recluse spider bite in 1980.

But the hump had got even bigger. I, who had unfond memories of hearing Dad shout me out of bed at 4 A.M. to milk when I was a boy, was now the caretaker of a bunch of bovine children—for to Dad, that's what they were. Indeed, Mom had often accused him of caring more for his livestock than for his family.

And so the winter, a hard, cold, muddy one, had dragged on. Every morning I walked down to load the forty- to fifty-pound bales, an exercise no doctor would recommend for a sedentary man my age. But he was dad, and I was son, and it was my duty. So why, after a few weeks, did I think the drudgery would never end—and why did I resent Dad's casual acceptance of my free labor at a task I hated?

On that Thursday morning, with the wind a searing blowtorch, I hated those cows with every fiber of my being. My self-pity was running high, and so was my temper. Dad had *said* he would do things I suggested—like keeping his old truck garaged during the fierce cold, or ordering more firewood. Then he wouldn't. On this morning, I called ahead and was told that the truck had started—but it hadn't. It had an old battery, another sore point. It's Dad's way or no way, which made me feel twelve all over again—and I'd grown to hate the feeling over the past dreary weeks.

We fed from the barn, which sat on a small slope, rolling the bales down the slope and breaking and tossing them. He didn't toss, I did. The cows rushed in, including the wickedly horned ones Dad "likes to look at."

"And be gored by?" I once said sourly.

"Aw, you worry too much," he growled.

I broke a bale near the barn and kicked it, in a hurry to escape the horns and hooves. Dad saw it and shouted, "Get it offa that hill! Them cows'll fall down."

It was the match that lit my fuse, and all the frustrations of past weeks exploded. "You and your blankety-blank *blank-blank* cows!" I roared. "What the hell's the matter with you? They have four legs and you have two—and I worry about *you* falling, not some damned steer!"

I was furious, because the ice was slick as slime, and indeed, Dad had earlier fallen on it. You don't take many ice-falls at seventy and keep walking away. It was another thing to fret about.

Dad's own temper rose with an eagerness that showed that here, at least, was someone he could do some discussing with—stress the second syllable of discussing. The air that was blue with cold became purple with profanity. Near the barn were he stood, icicles melted from the eaves—for when it came to cussing, my old man could shame a sailor. He bellowed that he didn't need me, and I roared, "Fine!"

I meant it and he meant it, for ten weeks of enforced together-ness—in the cause of his cows—had given me stress pains and wor-ries about my own health. To my parents I would forever be young and strong, no matter how old and gray I got, and I resented it. I was willing to feed, shelter, and care for them when old—but I wasn't willing to be a free farm laborer to keep their place going! They had good Social Security and a paid-for farm. Let them sell out and retire, as they should have when they were sixty-five!

Thus I fumed as I skidded icily back home. But conscience is an unrelenting tyrant. I knew I'd be back in the morning. I'd have to see his herd through the winter. Then, sad though it would be, Dad would have to make other arrangements.

Why, then, did I feel such terrible guilt?

✿ ✿ ✿

Ozark highways are narrow and two-laned, dipping deep into swales like asphalt roller coasters, zooming up over the hills—actions that cause tickles of delight in the spines of children. My sons hoot and holler at such times. These dipsy-doodle rides are high points when they visit me from California.

But after dusk, all asphalt seems to merge into the night, and you ride headlight beams that pull you into a rushing tunnel of darkness. You race along, out of touch with the world around you. Then suddenly you top a rise and find the world not only there, but lit by a moon so huge and golden it could almost be a flying saucer.

That's what happened to me one recent night near New Bethel Church, a scene of many a revival. I whizzed over a hill—and into a scene of indescribable beauty.

New Bethel is a small, plain church that looks out over a cemetery holding veterans from the Civil War and every war since. The fields extending away from it hold farm houses, barns, trees, and chicken houses—not to mention motionless herds of cud-chewing cows, lying like bundles on the ground. All of these were silvered by nature's night-light and looked as sharply defined as though it were day.

On yet another full-moon night, I saw a glowing sickle cutting a semicircle in the sky. Then it ballooned into view, a huge yellow orb bent on swallowing my hurtling pickup. I was saved by a solitary pasture oak, which reached its limbs up and snared the moon as a cat would catch a golden ball.

I braked, pulled to the side, and watched the moon's struggles to get free. It did, finally, and—flushed brighter by the wrestling match—climbed to new heights.

Full moons have several names in the Ozarks. Hunter's Moon and Hound Dog Moon are two of the most common. The former has to do with pursuing, through creek bottoms, brambles, and water if it gets in the way, the ever-present, ever-rascally raccoon.

In recent years, decadence has tinged the Ozarks as it has the rest of America, and now coon hunters hunt from the heated cabs of pickups or 4WDs, stopping the vehicles every so often to listen for the baying of the hounds, which often range a mile or more ahead of the hunters. Hound-dog men know from experience when a coon is treed. The dog's bay takes on a wilder, more frantic sound.

But coons have more than an even chance. They are probably the smartest animal in the woods. Scarred old veterans elude hounds more often than not, leaping thirty feet and more to the top of another tree. Then, like orangutans in the Borneo jungle, they slip quietly down and away. And it goes without saying that since water is one of their favorite habitats, they'll lose their scent—and the racketing dogs—by walking or swimming away in a stream.

Hunting and trapping of coons and certain other wildlife are done during the winter months so the fur won't slip. Only pelts tightened by frost have any value.

Trapping is more than a modest industry in the Ozarks, where in any given season many thousands of furs taken from coons, foxes, skunks, possums, minks, and bobcats are processed. As an industry, it is carefully regulated by the Missouri Department of Conservation.

Trapping is increased when animal populations reach pesty proportions, or there are so many that food isn't adequate to feed them. In Arkansas's famed rice country, beavers have tunneled levees and ruined thousands of acres of rice-growing lands. Trappers are always welcomed in such circumstances.

For a long time, I was anti-trapping. But that was before I had walked a mile in the shoes of many a poor hill family—to whom winter furs, which they labor hard for, can mean the difference between a Christmas for their kids and no Christmas at all. As long as a reasonable balance of nature is preserved by careful game management (and Missouri's is one of the best), there really should not be any outcries. But some folks will outcry anybody, just to be out crying. They would not complain if they had to live hand-to-mouth, like some Ozarkians do.

Coons are more than just smart—they're also dangerous. A few years ago, I was on a seven-day canoeing trip with a group from Wilderness Southeast, a Savannah, Georgia, non-profit organization that takes families into the woods and teaches them wilderness lore and respect for the environment. We canoed through the beautiful Okefenokee Swamp and one night camped on an ancient levee pincushioned by trees and thick undergrowth.

About midnight, the camp was awakened by the most god-awful screeching and snarling we'd ever heard. Two boar coons were locked in battle over garbage we thought we'd secured by tying it to the high pole of the rain tarp.

We yelled, and scared them off.

But it should be remembered that wild coons are so powerful, they can often kill a hound one-on-one—and some Ozark coon hounds are worth thousands of dollars apiece.

Many years ago, a reporter wrote, "An Ozarkian's wealth is mostly dogs."

That's still pretty true. That, and a full moon to hunt by.

❧ ❧ ❧

I heard Dad's voice as I came over the small rise north of the barn. He was crooning to Buster the bull, who came for a grain ration every morning, and to an old roan cow. "Old Polly's gonna have a bite with ya," Dad said, his voice as full of affection as that of someone petting a dog. "Yes sir, she's been watchin' you gettin' this here free grain, and she wants her share." The three stood by a wooden trough in the muddy corral.

How many times I had witnessed such sights in the years since I'd come back to the Ozarks. And, in recent months, how often I had hoped that Dad would realize his inability to keep up the old home place.

He would be seventy on his birthday. His heart bypass had not helped him as much as he'd hoped, and many thousands of dollars later he was on medication to keep him going. As he had told me on my last visit, "If I had it to do over again, I wouldn't do it. All that pain and money and I'm right back where I started."

When my sister, Glenda, had come from California to visit Dad, his cardiologist had refused to discuss the case with her. Doctors are no happier than anyone else when something they recommend doesn't pan out.

After haying the herd, we went into the house for coffee. Somehow, the old two-story bungalow looked especially forlorn on this cloudy pre-spring day. Dad's farm was probably first settled 150 years ago. Now it covers seventy-two acres of rolling permanent pasture—fenced, with a patch of woods and a couple of stock ponds. The small one by the outbuildings is spring fed. It's a pretty place, almost quaint.

A log barn built around 1910 was on the place when Dad bought it, but rot had set in and the dangerous old structure had to be removed. Now his barn is a sixty-by-forty-foot former chicken house that holds his winter hay, fourteen hundred bales, about a third raised in his central pasture. He built a sixty-foot loafing shed three years ago, adding to the house's living room at the same time. Like most family farms, this one is well-crafted, sturdy, and plain. Only to me, "plain" means it has character.

Mom had their warm morning wood stove cranked up pretty good, so the big living room was hot. With the livestock fed, and the weather too bad for much else, they would spend the morning watching television or reading. Mom loves the lurid "detective" magazines and cluck-clucks disapprovingly at every awful page of stories like "Sex Virgins in the Swamp Beast's Lair." A pile of *National Enquirer*s rests nearby, given to her regularly by another elderly farm wife.

"I'm sellin' out," Dad said suddenly.

I didn't think I had heard him right, and I said, "You're what?"

"I've had all I can take," he said, speaking as he always did without inflection, his voice amazingly deep to be coming from such a slight man. His face betrayed nothing of the war I knew was raging inside him. Here it was at last—the final bowing to the inevitable, the melancholy knowledge that his life was facing another bend in the road, perhaps its final one.

I studied the rug for a moment, unwilling to look at him. I had often voiced my wishes about his selling, yet now that he had made up his mind to do so, pictures flashed into my mind of him and Mom in a retirement home. Not here, in their own living room, surrounded by their own things—but in a strange place, among strangers.

"What will you do?" I asked finally.

"I don't have any ideas on that yet," Dad replied. "I ain't thought about it much."

My eyes strayed out the window to the small chicken house due east of the bungalow. Wind-ruffled chickens, fat and ready for spring, scratched and squawked behind wire thick with dried morning glory vines. Except for forty years, they could've been the same chickens in the same chicken yard on the old Charley Pokero place where we first farmed on the shares in 1945.

"Well," I said, "let me know how I can help."

Mom said nothing. Her eyes were fixed on the wall as if her thoughts were a thousand miles away. Perhaps they were, gazing at her favorite vista—the time so many years ago when she and Dad, vigorous, young, and full of dreams, had first charted their restless life together.

I found myself wishing the sun would shine. If the sun would only shine, we would all feel less like crying.

🌱 🌱 🌱

The city of Anderson lies in a low, sloping depression between two mountains. It really hasn't changed noticeably in a century. Old photos hanging in the bank still show much the same business area. Population has grown, but it's still under fifteen hundred. In fact, I would rather call Anderson a hamlet, but this understandably goes against the grain of the city fathers—perhaps because they don't wish to be known as "hamlet fathers."

During the holidays that mark the close of one year and its events, and open another year with its dreams, Anderson and all the surrounding towns strut their glitter and gloss as finely as St. Louis ever could. Indeed, we have an advantage. It would take all day to appreciate seasonal decorations in St. Louis, whereas in Anderson we can do so, quite cozily, in ten minutes—weather permitting.

The weather doesn't always allow leisurely strolls from the top of one hill to the top of another, and few folks walk that far anyway. Main Street sits in the bottom of the bowl, glittering like sugar grains, and that's where the action is.

But wintertime is also a time of savage rains. During a good old-fashioned gully-washer, the sky dumps water like an upended cauldron. Such was the case—many years before I came to the town—in Anderson.

Every place has at least one Great Flood, unless it's in the middle of the Sahara, and Anderson's was just before World War II. Beaver Branch, the tiny stream that cuts the town in half to join up at Town

Hole with Indian Creek, got completely out of bounds and washed out the bridge just west of the post office. Trying to track the exact date of the flood wasn't easy.

"I think it was just before I went into the service," said Tommy Dalton, a retired sailor. Tommy works for Bill Barnes in the L. L. Barnes Appliance Store a hundred feet west of the bridge. The store building has been there since at least World War I and was once a livery stable. During the flood, its lower rooms were muddied but weren't washed out.

Tommy suggested I check with Charlie McKenzie, who ought to be made the town's honorary historian. He had an idea Tommy was close on the flood. Nate Roark thought the same. "Tommy couldn't get back to East Anderson that night," Nate said, "so him and his pals spent the night with us." Roark owns a service station on Highway 71 West.

Tommy enlisted in 1941, so the flood might have been that winter. Beaver Branch, normally tiny, grew like a boa constrictor in a penful of pigs. Soon it was a swollen brown lake, with hundreds of feet separating its far shore from the post office that ordinarily sat just a few yards east. (The problem lay with Indian Creek, which creates Town Hole.)

When I called Nate on the telephone, he put the question to some others with him. I heard a woman holler, "What in the world does he want t'know that for? It's done and done." Folks who have lived their lifetimes in little towns take different views of events from those of outsiders. But to me, the tiny Ozark towns are both time-capsules and archaeological sites.

Other floods (none so severe as the one in 1941) have cut away at the limestone-and-dirt stream banks, occasionally uncovering curious relics from the past. Over a century, fill-dirt and debris were dumped along Beaver Branch to create more building space or replace soil chewed away by the waters. Five years ago, the partial chassis of a wrecked car from the 1920s came to view.

There was a flood alert recently as waters rose after a three-inch rain. But mostly the bridges and low-water bridges stood firm. However, all the streams were heavily swollen, as was Indian Creek, which slowly carves a limestone bluff ever nearer the hill on which sits the old, dignified Anderson Baptist Church. The waters still have a long way to go, and homes will topple before the church does, but within the next century, if the town is still here, who knows? Folks may have to do some more filling.

As with high winds and storms, I'm fascinated when nature flexes her muscles and shows her feminist side. She is no lady at such times; she is woman, hear her roar—and I stand above the flood looking down as rushing water erodes ever more earth, making the river brown and thick as gravy. At such times, I murmur a parody of the seventy-first quatrain from "The Rubaiyat of Omar Khayyam":

> The moving water eats and having et,
> Moves on, nor all thy piety nor wit,
> Shall lure it back to put back half a pound
> Of soil it's taken from this mountain town.

❊ ❊ ❊

I stepped out of Dad's house into a night blacker than the ace of spades—no moon, no stars, no lights anywhere.

Then the sheet lightning started, like the footprints of the gods, coated with fire. And with each great rippling tapestry of light, there came accompanying thunder. Strange. It did indeed sound like the distant noise of ninepins being played by Rip Van Winkle's gnomes, high in the Catskills of three hundred years ago.

Dad waits out his time, staying home mostly, doing little but watching mindless television reruns. To get him to visit me, I either have to drag him bodily or tell him one of his dogs is living on my porch. He and Mom, after forty-eight years together, now live apart again. All these stresses and strains, just at a time when his age and health make him least able to withstand them, are taking their toll.

Each rippling sheet of lightning showed how high the clouds were piled, transforming their innards into dark caverns lit by torches that burned for only a moment—heavenly fire at its finest.

"Sure looks like rain," I hollered back in to Dad.

"Well, we need it," he yelled back, "I hope it comes a duck-drowner."

The wind rose as I drove home and was whipping the huge walnut trees like feather-dusters by the time I reached the trailer. Flashes of lightning showed the yellow ribs of two-by-fours set by the carpenter I'd hired to take on the task of bringing new life to an ancient dwelling. I had known the problems we'd encounter—but that's a tale for another time.

Walnut trees are mixed blessings at best. Beautiful to look at, they're mainly fakers. Their leaves come last and leave first, and all year long they fall like green-and-gold snow, while the nuts themselves seem to become fist-sized overnight—and can deliver near-lethal blows. Now nuts, leaves, and a variety of branches littered the ground. As I streaked for the door, a terrific crash of lightning hit the huge old oak by my gate, one hundred feet distant, pulverizing a thick upper limb and sending its shards crashing to earth.

When lightning or age finally brings that oak to its end, I'm certain a count of its rings will show that the acorn it came from first hit the rocky Ozark soil when Yankee and Rebel were killing each other on Pea Ridge Battlefield, just a few miles from where the tree now stands. Dad removed one of similar size in his yard a year ago—lightning-struck, it had stood, skeletal and gray, for two years, and he feared it might fall. The local light company felled it close to the ground, and I counted 110 rings—some so narrow, the years they represented must have had terrible droughts.

The gnomes with their ninepins were striking fire with each impact. The wind howled like a million lost souls, bending the trees like stalks of grass. I had barely closed the trailer door when rain slammed the earth in a Niagara-sized flood. As lightning sculptured golden trees in the sky, I flipped on the TV and watched the steady march of letters warning that tornadoes were expected in the area, and viewers should go to a place of shelter.

A place of shelter. For twelve years, I'd trusted to luck to fend off the more deadly of the elements. I knew what a tornado could do—not just to a mobile home, favorite target of sensationalist TV cameras, but even to reinforced masonry buildings.

I, though, have no storm cellar, no place of shelter. If it's my time, I'll go. If it's the old oak tree's last moment on earth, it will fall. And Dad . . . well, he's known for a long time that his clock is winding down.

So is everyone's. We are so mortal, so fragile—and still we proceed as if we will live forever. Perhaps if more of us really accepted that we must truly die someday, we'd live better lives for every day that follows the reading of this line.

Perhaps.

❁ ❁ ❁

The phone rang and I picked it up to hear a familiar voice.

"Chilly?"

"Bo?"

"Is this Chilly?"

"Is this Bo Harmon?"

"Yeah. Y'wanna go coon huntin'?"

"Right now?" I hadn't had any dinner, but I'd told Bo Harmon that I wanted to relive the enchanted scenes of my boyhood, when—fourteen and full of spirit—I had sailed through nights of coon-hunting splendor. That was how I remembered it from thirty-seven years later anyhow.

Bo said he was leaving right away, so I jumped in my pickup and lit out for his home in Anderson. He was loading his two coon hounds into a portable kennel when I got there. The oldest, a bluetick named Okie, was his best. Bo was matching Okie up with Queenie, a less experienced Tennessee walker bitch.

"We'll go over t'ards Southwest City," he said, "to a farm near the Oklahoma line. Lotsa creeks, trees an' brush there—an' I've got quite a bunch o' coons outta there." He paused, looked up at the tree tops swaying against the star-frosted sky. "Wind's gettin' up some, though. Just hope it don't get up much higher—it'll blow the smell away."

"Spoor."

"What?"

"Spoor means smell."

"Oh." Bo busied himself locking the dogs in, his every move showing he already wondered about inviting an armchair coon hunter. Soon we were headed out Highway 71. Thirty minutes later, Bo steered his pickup off a dirt road chuckholed by recent rains and parked it deep in some woods. He released the dogs, and they started sniffing dead logs, the bases of huge oaks, brush, and winter leaves.

The bluetick whined, whipped his quirt of a tail. Queenie said, "Roo?" and suddenly both of them vanished.

For a long time we stood amid the trees. Thick vines writhed in the wind that moaned in the branches. Tiny chirps struck my ears.

"Hear those night birds?" I asked Bo.

"Them's limbs rubbin' t'gether."

"Oh."

The sky was a black cloth sprayed with silver paint. Never had I seen so many stars. I looked at Bo's chunky form. At sixty-seven, he's in better shape than most men of thirty. He smokes, though, saying every time he lights up, "These damn cigarettes'll kill a man." Yet through muddy fields and over fences, through thorns and over creeks, he never slowed.

"WaROOO! WaROOO!" Far away, hard to hear against the wind, came the voice of Okie. Coon hounds speak mostly in French horn—the *trompette de casse* that signaled pursuit in medieval times. I wondered if Bo knew Europe had coon-type critters called raccoon dogs from which fur was sold, just as fur is sold from American raccoons. Such speculation was silly—especially since we were headed full-tilt toward the sounds. We reached the base of two old oaks. Bo took one look at the trees, and at his hounds rooing at them, and said disgustedly, "Hell, they're holler."

We walked the dogs a quarter mile so they could find a new scent. Off they raced, and we went after. Let me assure you right now that if you can coon hunt, even if you are ninety, then you can get into the commandos. The ranks of greenbriars alone can stop armored trucks, and when I scampered over a woven-wire fence and straddled some, they stopped me. I quickly re-scampered and came down elsewhere, perfuming the woods with some mighty fragrant phrases.

The dogs, at least, were having a wonderful time—and I think Bo was, too. Once, in a spooky grove of twisted trees we came upon a cow graveyard. Skeleton after skeleton glowed in the gloom, some still tented in leathery hides—sepulchers of skin stretched over rib rafters.

"This feller lost quite a few cows," Bo observed as he stopped and lit a cigarette. "WaROOOOO!" howled Okie, and we were off again, splashing across creeks, sinking into muddy pastures, being whipped by briars and branches. Funny, I didn't remember it being like this during my kidhood. But my body had been pliant, then, whereas now it was plywood.

These procedures went on for several hours and miles. At last I'd had it and, hoping I wouldn't hurt Bo's feelings, told him I was ready to go home if he was.

"I'm ready," Bo said. Luckily, the hounds were snuffling nearby and were easily leashed. We walked down Stateline Road, talking about coons Bo had got in his life. "I'd hate t'make a guess how many," he said. "But one night over near Nevada, I got seventeen." Furs can bring as much as twenty-five dollars apiece.

We walked on toward the truck a mile away. I talked to Bo from Oklahoma, he responded from Missouri, and the hounds walked the line.

❧ ❧ ❧

There have been many snows in my life. Some have been bitter, and some have been beautiful. In one, caught far from home on the Oklahoma plains, I came within an ace of freezing to death.

But on this December night something had awakened me, some signal from the past, some kind of paternal alarm clock. I walked in my underwear (O, long johns, of thee I sing) through the cold trailer and stopped in the hallway to peer out the small window. My watch said 3 A.M.

Outside, there was a scene of pure magic. The walnut grove was thickly frosted with snow. My truck looked like a mock-up carved from soap, and the bare limbs of walnuts, elms, and oaks were wrapped in bandages of airy whiteness.

It was the first snow of the year, a lonely, lovely picture that took me back seventeen years to a night in Iowa City, Iowa—and a head-long rush at 3 A.M. to the University of Iowa hospital. The little VW roared through the early-morning darkness, its worn-out muffler announcing its passage to the sleeping city.

It had snowed thickly that April night in 1967. The huge old elms, even then gradually dying of Dutch elm disease, lined the route like a phalanx of angels. The road had been partly cleared of snow, but it was still slick—and I was grateful for the engine in the back of the little car, which seemed to add stability.

Beside me, my first wife, Rose Marie, gripped the handle on the dash, looking like a statue carved from darkness. I could not even see her, swollen with the child that—half an hour earlier—had announced its intention to be born. It was our first, and if it hadn't been for the covering dark, we would both have looked pale and tense.

Outside my trailer, the snow filtered down. The yard with its woven-wire fence rolled on down a slope into a small hillside of woods. Under the daddy of all my walnut trees, just south of the treehouse, lay a lumpy, snow-covered sculpture—a helter-skelter pile of old saw blades, plow seats, and wheels from long-vanished farm wagons and plows. Winter had turned it into art.

Rosie and I wanted a house, but we never got it, not during our entire twelve-year marriage. In graduate school, we lived in a series of shacks owned by a female slumlord whose vicious temperament resulted in the students calling her The Shark of Iowa City. She is dead now, years dead, and Iowa City is bigger and uglier. But she is part of its folklore. Wherever she is, I hope it's very high in Fahrenheits.

We wheeled into the hospital parking lot, and I helped Rosie through the foot-deep snow into the lobby. My telephone call had alerted the nurses. Soon my wife was being wheeled toward a room where her yawning obstetrician, Dr. Mulvaney, waited with a sleepy smile.

"Scared, Honey?" I asked as she rode.

"Yes," she said in a small, tight voice.

"Me too," I said, feeling that somehow it was the wrong thing to say.

Dr. Mulvaney and the nurses positioned her on a gurney. Her abdomen had lengthened and flattened. The fetus had already begun lining up for the birth. Painful contractions had started.

Dr. Mulvaney let me kiss her, then shooed me out as he prepared a hypodermic for an injection. I would not see Rosie again for three hours, during which time I would wait in a small, empty room, out of sight of the nurses (who had other things to do than watch me pace). From its window, I watched the falling snow. The tiny, whirling flakes that had escorted us to the hospital were fatter now, and falling thicker. I didn't know it, but we were on the edge of a snowfall of historic proportions.

At some point, unable to bear it, filled with a nameless fear, I went to the nurses' station. One of them reassured me—just as a banshee shriek filled the corridors.

"That isn't *your* wife," the nurse said. I didn't know whose wife it was, but I felt sorry for her. (She was fine; her baby was a twelve-pounder.)

On a blackboard suspended above the station, Dr. Mulvaney, a bit of a humorist, had chalked in my name. I looked and did a double-take. It read "Childless."

Even as I read it, a nurse came out of the delivery room undoing her mask. With a broad smile, she erased "Childless" and chalked in "Childress Boy." All the nurses were grinning, watching my reaction, knowing that each new father reacted differently—some fainting, some shouting, some running out wordless and returning hours later.

"A boy," I said. There was a goofy grin on my face. "A *boy*."

The nurse took me in. My son was atop his weary, drowsy mother, still wet from birth. They lay together among the white sheets, like works of art in snow.

❧ ❧ ❧

Six below zero and no wind chill. I could only imagine what it would be if a wind sprang up. It had already been one of the coldest nights in this area's history—eleven below on my porch thermometer when I went to bed at one A.M. I had kept my faucets dripping all night, and electric lights burning under my rocked-in trailer. Now, at seven A.M., at least I had water for coffee and cooking.

I had risen to a beautiful dawn, with the eastern sky forge-red and brightening—like metal reaching its peak of hotness before being hammered into tools. The contrast was not so deceptive. Touching bare metal at six below zero could burn like a branding-iron.

The porch creaked under my feet, unable to expand its planks without protest. In one past winter, before I re-planked the porch, I came out to find one plank with a three-foot split. Enough water had seeped into the weathered board so that when a quick freeze brought ice, the growing crystals cracked the board as surely as a wedge cleaves a log.

Looking eastward to the borders of Dad's pastureland, I saw nothing but white dunes of snow, an occasional oak left by the dozer when the land was cleared (ranchers always take out too many trees, trying for that extra mouthful of grass for their cattle), and the great oak grove that twists like a blacksnake over the curving pastures.

The grove borders Dad's land and is for sale. I wish I had the money to buy it—it is virgin woodland, and in this country where rich ranchers and poor farmers compete for vanishing pasture, it's just a matter of time until someone with short-term profits in mind destroys all those trees.

I am not a raving ecologist by any means. But trees are something special—and something terribly vital. If we cut more than we plant, and that seems true almost everywhere, there could come a time when the atmosphere—which depends on greenery to replenish the oxygen supply—will be so thin we will gasp our way to death like fishes out of water.

The kettle was whistling inside, a shrill sound that couldn't be ignored. Coffee, rich with Carnation milk and brown sugar, is all the breakfast I could afford, calorie-wise. Weeks of snow and zero temperatures had kept me from my morning walks.

As I rose and placed my coffee cup in the sink, a piercing racket came from outside the kitchen window—the voice of a bird, impossible to describe, yet unmistakably merry. Easing quietly onto the porch, I peered upwards to where the upper limbs of my walnut trees etched their bones against the blue sky.

There, far up in the top of one, sat an oddly shaped bundle of feathers, alternately pecking at the limbs and lifting its head to give forth a grating warble. What could it possibly find in those barren crevices to sustain it—and why hadn't it flown south with all the other birds? And, in all this frigid sterility, what in the world could it find to sing about with such cheeriness?

It hadn't flown south because for the junco—the bob-tailed little muff I was watching—this is the south. It winters in the Ozarks, somehow finding enough seeds to survive (much easier when there is no snow). But prolonged snows can doom this member of the sparrow family—and probably all that kept this one alive now were the ginberries on the juniper tree I'd planted years ago.

Not being a bird watcher, I didn't know any of this until I called my friends Joan and Hac Yeagley in Stella. Their riverbank home is a bird hotel in the winter, because they put out birdseed in many suspended houses—watching the flocks of cardinals, bluejays, juncos, and bluebirds from their breakfast window. They know a lot about birds. They know a lot about living, too, having lived in a tent for two fierce winters a decade ago while they and their children built their Ozarks home.

The sun lolled above the horizon, a stickless red lollipop. As I turned back inside, the junco spotted my movements and flew to a safer tree. I put some breadcrumbs out on the well-house—they were all I had until I could get to town when the thick drifts had melted.

Inside, the sun turned a frost-covered window into a glittering universe.

Those diamonds might not be forever, but until the sun's rays made them vanish, they were more beautiful than any of Ford's or Rockefeller's.

❧ ❧ ❧

There was a time when I knew my firstborn son, Christopher. The evidence is in the pictures that lie before me as I write. Rosie, my first wife, recently called from California. Chris, not quite eighteen, had gone joy riding with another boy. The trouble was, it wasn't their car. They brought it back, yet it was only the kindness of the owners that kept the boys from being jailed.

I think back to the several summers that have come and gone, summers that Chris loved because he could spend them in the Ozarks. Summers full of swimming, canoeing, and fishing.

Chris loved to fish. He had an uncanny talent for it, too. Fish seemed to love his hooks, no matter what the bait, and there never was a time when he didn't put me to shame. It was strange, too, how he could show infinite patience to some bass or catfish lolling beneath the ripples. But the bright, clear Ozark streams seemed to have a calming effect on him that city asphalt never could.

The last time I saw my son, he was the size of a grown man—and remarkably handsome. He had shared in equal measure my blond looks and his mother's dark Armenian beauty. I was in California only for a brief time, on business, and was able to spend only part of a day with him. Sometimes jobs and careers rob us of so much.

Even then, he confessed to having trouble in school—this from a boy with a very high I.Q. He wanted to drop out but was forbidden to do so. Only much later did we find out he was simply refusing to show up for classes. His California teachers did not inform his mother until it was too late for him to make up the work.

He didn't want to anyway, I was told. (I got all this by long-distance phone.) He was coming up to his eighteenth birthday—freedom day, or so he thought. By the time it came around, he was too far behind in all his courses. And so he didn't graduate from high school. When the rest of his classmates walked between the rows of people to take their diplomas, Chris was somewhere in the city, having left home because his actions had caught up with him and shattered his world.

I'm looking at a picture now. It is of Chris undersized at fourteen, gazing across Grand Lake past a sunken old highway bridge usually hidden by the brown waters. But the lake is low in the picture. He stands, a small silhouette, rod and creel in his hands, looking into infinity. How small and beautiful he looks, my absent son, my troubled boy. The heaviness in my chest won't go away.

In another picture, he is twelve, clad in bib overalls. His unruly brown hair is uncombed as always. A white rabbit is tucked inside the bib, and he's gazing fondly at it. There was nothing moody about him then—he was just a kid, unaware that he was growing into turbulence and pain, into frustration and puzzlement as all his hormones began announcing themselves.

These photographs are worth more than gold to me. I can't understand people who never take pictures, because how else can a life that is past be brought back again?

In my files are many pictures of summers with my sons. I have old, stiffened rolls of Kodak movie film—thin 8 mm strips of their growing years. When I cast them on a screen, there is magic and mystery, for where are the tiny bundles that once rolled on the rug with kittens and pups? Can they still be locked inside my three contributions to the human race? If they are, I'm glad. But if they are not, my sons can come to their own archives, any time they choose, and stare once again at the beginnings of their journey through life.

❧ ❧ ❧

The little heifer lay in quiet agony in a briar patch, her neck locked and rigid from the terrible contractions that racked her starved body. Life had not been kind to her. Neither had this calf, her first, for it refused to be born.

"I don't know how she got such a big calf in 'er," whined the mousy little farmer who owned the heifer. "All I kinda figure is she got outa the pasture an' got over with that big ol' Limosine bull my neighbor has."

Piecemeal farmers like this one are secretly glad when a cow from their scruffy herd, usually with help from a dilapidated fence, gets bred to a good bull for free.

They are the Pa Kettles of this world, always on the verge of starving out—always on the alert for anything they can get for nothing. The vet, for instance, is one of their favorite targets—for if they pay him at all it is usually months after the work has been done.

This time, however, the free breeding had backfired. So small a cow should never have been matched with so large a bull. And this was obviously the man's best heifer—or had been. Now she lay dying because she couldn't deliver the oversized calf.

I had come by the vet's early that morning from dropping mail in the box outside the post office. Like me, he was always up early. We were good friends and enjoyed an occasional cup of coffee before the phone's endless jangling woke the sparrows nesting under his roof edge.

It was not to be. The phone rang, the vet answered and his face fell—a sign that an unwanted or unfavorite customer was on the line. When he hung up, he asked if I wanted to ride along. "We can take our coffee cups," he said. "I've got ring-holders."

Several times during the ride, the vet expressed the hope that there wouldn't be a C-section waiting for him at the other end. A field

Caesarean in mud and cold is hard on the animal and torment for the vet—whose hands often break open afterwards from contact with weather and the cow's fluids.

Now it seemed that it would not only be a C-section, but that the cow might not make it. She had obviously been lying in pain for long hours.

"Why didn't you call me earlier?" the exasperated vet asked. It is the worst and most often-repeated sin of farmers—calling late.

"I checked her this morning," the owner said. "She was OK then, but tonight I got back an' here she was, all stretched out like this."

Off to one side lay a barbaric T-shaped device, a store-bought calf-puller.

"Did you try pulling the calf with that?" the vet asked.

Glancing nervously at the eight-foot-long aluminum girder, the man licked his lips and said, "Yeah, I give it a try."

The vet would never say anything, for he is a kindhearted man. But I knew what he was thinking. Such devices in the hands of "barnyard vets" needlessly kill many cows. A calf too large to pass the pelvic opening, literally winched through by farmers with no training at all, can kill both mother and offspring.

"Did you position the head, like I showed you last time?"

"Uh . . ." The farmer looked away, spat an amber tobacco stream and kicked at a briar root. "I . . . well, I guess I fergot."

The vet was down on his side in the water of birth, his arm inside and searching. Withdrawing, he said the fetus was too large to go through the breech. "A C-section is our only hope," he told me.

The farmer went off to one side and began offering prayers, his lips silently moving. It is an age-old remedy. In the years before veterinarians, prayers that were believed able to move mountains sometimes could not call forth calves that would not be born. Either way, it was the Lord's will. Or the devil's curse.

From the moment the vet told the farmer a Caesarean section was the only hope, the farmer delivered sermons.

"I used t'be a drunkard," he said emotionally. "But the Lord saved me from it. I drink iced tea, now."

"That's wonderful, sir," I said—for it truly was. A little common sense would have helped, too, but being saved from alcoholism was extremely worthwhile. I smiled. He smiled back.

An hour later—weary from cutting open and sewing up the thick hide of a cow and extracting a huge calf—the vet stumbled to his feet. Both cow and calf had a fighting chance, now. (I later found out that despite the primitive spot, the briars, mud, and cold, both animals survived, no small miracle in itself.)

"You know," the vet said, as we sped homeward, "I'm certainly willing to grant that prayers and sermons are godly in nature. But it's got to be the devil that makes *amateurs* try to *preach!*"

❊ ❊ ❊

I n 1949, my family sharecropped the old Reed place near Marlow, Oklahoma, off the paved road two miles on red gumbo clay that in muddy weather clung to tires like glue. It took high-wheeled vehicles to get through when it rained, like Dad's 1946 Chevy pickup. That pickup was like new for a truck, and he was as proud of it as a kid is of a Christmas toy.

South of us, half a mile, lived the Bledsoes. And if ever anybody was poorer than Ronny and Elma Lee Bledsoe, I don't know who it was. We were poor, but in contrast to the Bledsoes, we were practically millionaires. We had several cows, some pigs, chickens, lots of home-canned food in the cellar, an old but good John Deere tractor, and, of course, the pickup.

Ronny worked for old man Johnson for a dollar a day and a furnished shack. He had little but the clothes on his back and certainly could not dream of owning a car. But he and Elma Lee were young and strong, full of that optimism youth is so noted for, and they did have a little boy to help make their life complete.

Ronny Jr. was only a year old when, crawling in the yard while his mother scrubbed clothes on a washboard inside, he was bitten by a rabid dog. The beast had come slobbering and stumbling out of the woods, and in the throes of the dreaded scourge we called hydrophobia, it bit the child—even as Ronny, running up with his shotgun as Elma Lee screamed *"Mad dog, mad dog!"* shot the animal dead.

Ronny ran the half mile to Dad's with his baby son in his arms and his wife right behind. Dad almost never ate lunch at home when he was plowing the south forty, but on this day something had brought him home. He took one look at the baby's wound and the three of them jumped in the pickup. Elma Lee held her son all the way to Duncan—the only hospital for miles—and there he began the terribly painful series of vaccinations into the stomach that was his sole hope of survival.

"I can still hear that little boy's screams," my dad said not long ago, as we remembered the poverty of our past and the folks who shared it.

Little Ronny was bitten in September, and for weeks to come, Dad drove the Bledsoes the twenty-one miles to the hospital. Laboratory analysis had shown the dog to be rabid, so the boy had to have the Pasteur-invented vaccine every day for weeks, then reinforcing doses thereafter. The pain is agonizing, but rabies is an almost total killer without the shots.

Autumn came with its rains and falling leaves, but Dad's truck never failed to slither through the red clay and make it to the highway. Of course, he had tire chains, but it was a source of pride to him not to put them on unless he was stuck like a bug to flypaper. He just threw a few bales of hay in the back for weight and headed north to the highway.

Ronny Bledsoe, Jr., was bitten in late September and finished all his shots early in December. The vaccine had saved his life, but there had been side-effects; the child was weak and pale as Christmas week approached.

Dad and Mom knew the Bledsoes didn't have a dime for the poor-box, so when the holiday came—with our own crops laid by and most of our bills paid, at least paid for the year—they got together a Christmas basket.

It wasn't a whole lot, just some oranges, candy, and nuts. And there was a bright Raggedy Andy doll for little Ronny, who was now toddling precariously about the house, getting into as much mischief as his adoring parents would overlook—which was all of it.

Elma Lee brewed some coffee, gave the baby his present, and sat down to visit with my folks.

Finally, she said in a low, husky voice, "I reckon they ain't words to tell you how thankful we are to y'all."

"That's a mortal fact," her young husband said. "We're very much obliged."

"Well," Mom said, picking up the basket as we got ready to leave. "I'm just sorry it's such a poor Christmas, but maybe next year'll be better."

Elma Lee swept her baby up as he trundled past. Showering him with kisses and hugging him to her, she laughed and said, "Well Miz Childress, I know what you mean. But I reckon there just ain't no better Christmas than I'm holdin' right here in my arms!"

We left then. But as Dad walked past the front of the truck to drive us home, he grinned slightly and gave the hood an affectionate slap.

🕸 🕸 🕸

Folks in the Ozarks are generally more close-mouthed than most citizens—if you discount gossip.

However, down here gossip is still considered to be largely the province of women. When a man's mouth is open, there is usually a bottle of beer filling it. Men do talk, of course. They talk about a lot of things. They talk about cows, the health of cows, how to fix ailing cows, the market price of cows, and so forth.

They also talk about the weather. What kind of weather is best for cows, worst for cows, will drown or blow away cows, or cause screwworms in cows. If they talk about their wives at all, it is only to inquire whether they are taking good care of the cows.

I always thought my dad, who speaks only two or three times a year, was the epitome of the Quiet Ozarkian. But one day in Anderson, I met what appeared to be his match, and then some.

In southwestern Missouri, stores like Tatum's, Bell's, Western Auto, Village Variety, and Westco usually have post-Christmas sales. Those of us who don't have a hefty Christmas budget try to make up for it on these sales, especially as regards stuff like sheets, towels, and other household items. Often such merchandise is set up on the sidewalks along Main Street, and unless the weather is blowing a gale, folks turn out by the hundreds to loot and plunder merchants' wares at reduced prices.

I am in favor of such sidewalk sales and never miss one. With Christmas behind me, I was dodging among merchandise, and in and out of stores on a spending spree. With care, my seventeen dollars would go a long way.

It was while I was in Brady's Jewelry Store talking to Jeff Brady that I first saw the man. He stood on the sidewalk and stared at me. I left Brady's and went to another store. The fellow just kept looking at me. He was bone-thin, with a shallow, cavernous face and hollow eyes. I'd never seen him around Anderson before, and to tell the truth, the way he kept looking right at me made me nervous. I felt a cold chill, but went on to another merchant.

No matter who I chatted with, whenever I came back out on the sidewalk, the fellow was staring at me. Not saying a word, just standing, arms folded, gazing at me as if he'd never seen anything like me in the world before. What a frigid-looking character.

Once he broke with custom and rubbed a fist into his eye. I figured either a wasp had flown in there, or he was trying to clear his vision so he could see me better. Again came the cold chill, and this time, so help me, it seemed to blow right through me.

It was with genuine relief that I bumped into Charley McKinzie, who owns Bell's Drugstore. He was taking a break while his wife, Sonya, a watercolorist so good I've considered kidnapping her (only Charlie wouldn't ransom her), minded their goods. Charlie, along with the pipe that he has apparently had surgically implanted, would get me away from The Starer. As I have mentioned once or twice, Charley never says one word when twenty or thirty will do as well. Good ol' Charley! Salvation was just one of his sermons away.

"Hey, Charley, good to see you! I. . ."

"Sorry, Chilly, Jim needs my help in his store and I can't talk now." And he disappeared.

The bony man with the bare stare had taken a new post, this time leaning against the barber shop, which was closed for the occasion. Exasperated, I stared back at him—and again I felt that coldness, almost a wind, sweeping through my whole body. Damnation!

What on earth was it about this fellow that could produce such shivery feelings? True, it was a mighty cold day, with more than a breeze blowing—if a bit inconsistently. But I only felt chilled when I faced him, north of me, and when he looked at me with those expressionless eyes. And during all this time, he had never once uttered a word.

If the scoundrel knew me, why didn't he speak? If he didn't like me—impossible!—why didn't he come up and say so? Was he some long-lost relative? No, that couldn't be, for they have never been shy, and always show up at victualing time.

As the morning wore on, my nemesis kept up his staring at me. Right at me, full front. No sidling, no surreptitious gazes. The fellow was as brazen as a school bell. Without expression, without a sound, he continued to look at me, to stare at me, to bug the devil out of me *until I could stand it no longer!*

"Mister," I said, ignoring the shiver that shot through me as I headed towards him, "may I ask just why you have been staring at me all morning long?"

Startled by the energy in my tone, he drew himself up to his full height, and answered, "Well, sir, I reckon I was just wonderin' how long it'd take you t'realize that the whole front end o' your overalls is unbuttoned and has been for two hours. Ain't you been feelin' kinda drafty?"

❀ ❀ ❀

I saw Mom the other day. She sat in a car at a market, on the right side, which meant that someone—whether man or woman I could not tell—had driven her to the store.

There was one awful, frozen instant in which she recognized me, almost against her will—and then the mantle of anger descended across her face once more. She sat there, an old and lonely woman sunk like a pier in her bitterness. From it she drew strength, as she had for many years.

At some point in her life, Mom decided that men were the sole source of all her woes. The two men closest to her during these years of change were Dad and me—and I lived out of range, so Dad caught most of the hell her tongue and temper were capable of.

Finally, old and sick himself, Dad could take no more of the unending tirades, the senseless anger. He said either he or she would have to leave. Mom snapped at the chance, for Dad gave her half the value of the farm—as he should have—and she had been saving her money for years. Soon she was living in a comfortable, cheap apartment in federal housing for the aged.

When I saw her in the car, some dim stirring began inside me. I though how wonderful it would be if we could just roll back the years and the quarrels and the misunderstandings and be mother and son—not enemies—again. But her reaction was swift and predictable. I had tried many times to understand her, to placate her, to let her know that in spite of everything her family still loved her. But when she was drinking, her mind became twisted beyond fathoming.

I remember our first argument after I returned to the Ozarks. I could always tell when she'd dipped into her secret cache of liquor, although she was convinced she held it well. On that day, I berated her for drinking. Instead of the rage I would come to know, her face crumpled and a pair of tears trickled down her furrowed face. I put my arms around her.

"Aw, Mom, don't do that," I said. "I'm sorry I said anything."

She wiped away the tears on her apron, saying in a low voice, "You hate me, don't you Son?"

"No, Mom, I don't hate you," I said. "I'm just worried about your health is all."

We would never be that close again.

No son wants to hate his mother, but it's not an uncommon agony in our society—and, Lord knows, it is not new. There have been times when I thought sure I hated mine, that I could not tolerate another moment with her—for she had caused all her children much pain. But deep down, I know I love her—and pity her and feel sorrow for her.

After a lifetime of knowing her, I still don't know her. I only recognize that part of the demon in her has rubbed off on me—a snarling, amber genie crouched and waiting to leap if I am off guard for an instant. That's why I don't drink anymore.

Mom must know something is wrong. She tried religion for a while, but finally the Jehovah's Witnesses stopped coming, recognizing the power of the chemical that ruled her.

On this day, in the brilliant Ozark sun, seeing her there in the car with a mask for a face, my mind turned backward. And I was a boy again, crying with leg-ache in my attic room after a day in the fields that was much too long and hard for a ten-year-old. And I heard the stairs creak, and Mom coming up them in her worn old gown—to apply liniment to my aching limbs and pull the covers around me when the pain stopped, so I could sleep.

And the many times she fed us kids the lion's share of whatever meager meal we had in the cotton fields. And the time she saved my baby sister and me from death by fire in a shack in a slum in Phoenix, Arizona.

Nothing her demon can do can erase those memories.

Those memories are etched in my heart forever.

🙣 🙣 🙣

They've been called "The Boys" as long as I've known them, although they haven't been boys for over half a century.

They sat inside the house, watching the gray rain drumming against the old tin shed, watching the wind blow gusts through the giant oaks in the yard, out past the gate, out across the pasture—itself so wet it gleamed in the misty light.

Dad and Uncle Jack—Dad's sole remaining brother—had sat for two days, talking about things that matter only to them. Jack had driven up from Oklahoma to visit, to drink his daily twelve-pack of beer and lighten Dad's load with his dry, wry humor. Jack would have made a natural storyteller if things had been different. Instead, he's been a construction worker all his life.

Dad and Jack were the last two Childress boys born in a family that numbered thirteen. Four died at birth. But when Jack was born, the order was reversed, and his mother died of childbed fever. An old country doctor had forgotten to wash his hands, and a woman died. In 1922, in rural Oklahoma, such things happened.

Dad had seen his own father die; Jack had never seen either his father or his mother. Small wonder, then, that the seven-year-old and the infant would become the closest of all the brothers.

The Boys. I had gone to visit, of course, for I dearly love Jack's humor. I knew why he had come. His doctors had told him his own heart was showing the strain of too many cigarettes, too much drinking, too many hard years.

"Still smoking those cigars?" I chided him, and Jack said, "Why Bill, I need more of 'em—and more beer, too!"

"He's lily-pure now, Jack," Dad grunted. "You'll be lucky if he don't give you a sermon." Dad, too, had had a couple of beers. But he drinks so little, I was glad to see him do it.

Somehow, the feeling slowly came over me that I was intruding. Not in any rude way—it was just that I was a stranger to them now, for they were sharing things I could write about yet never know. And what they shared most was the ever-increasing knowledge of their mortality.

How strange to know that the inevitable must come; that a favorite uncle and a father you love are melting like wax into that final mold. That the years they were born in—1915 and 1922—are almost a lifetime away.

As I headed home across the flooded pastures, I remembered the oldest picture I have of Dad. He is standing barefooted, his toes curled in the dirt, his pants rolled up to expose skinny shins. He has a too-big cap perched on his head and an impish grin on his face, a grin I have never seen anywhere except in that old photograph.

How strange is the transition from that smiling seven-year-old to the man ten times older—from a stick clattering on a picket fence to a worn chair in a tumbledown farmhouse. At home I put my arm around Jason's shoulders.

"Son," I said. "Let's go look at some pictures I took of you when you were just a little boy."

And we did.

✤ ✤ ✤

My father watched his own father die in the kitchen of an Oklahoma farm house when he was six.

The coronary that killed George E. Rastus Childress was an alien thing that Dad didn't understand. All he knew, finally, was that his father wouldn't be coming in from milking his herd of Jerseys anymore to give him a playful swat before sitting down to breakfast. It was 1923.

Dad's father was forty-seven when he died at the kitchen table, slowly and gasping for each breath as a blow torch burned and expanded in his chest. He was the most successful farmer in the area at the time, with a large family consisting of seven sons and two daughters. His two oldest sons, watching in mute terror as he died, slowly massaged his feet, not knowing what else they could do.

Dad took it all in, his eyes round with fright and wonder. I have an old picture of him as he must have looked then, in trousers rolled to the knee and a tam o'shanter type of cap. His toes are bare, turned inward in the dust of a country road, a thin and smiling kid who now is a thin, unsmiling, very sick old man.

After they buried his father, they told Dad he'd gone to heaven. Dad didn't understand what they meant. They said George E. Rastus was an angel now, with wings like a bird, and watched over by God. George E. Rastus had raised his family to be devout Methodists.

But my dad still couldn't fathom what had happened. And when his mother, Sudie, a tiny, blond, very pretty woman, died of childbed fever the April after her husband's November death, Dad began walking around the big, empty old house—a small boy searching for his parents. Surely they were just hiding. Surely they were just playing some game.

I have often tried to imagine what lies deep in my father's mind. Lord, the things he must have buried there, layer upon layer, as life dealt him one blow after another. His home life was so bad he ran away forever at fourteen. He rode the rails and lived in hobo jungles.

He had a brief stint in the Army—and bought his way out with a loan from his brother, he hated it so much. He grew tall, handsome, and lean. Even today, at seventy, his hair is almost coal black—though bad health has begun the graying process. When I was four, he met and married my mother, staying with her for forty-eight years when most men would not have lasted a decade. What a mismatched pair to last for half a century.

But the layers, the protective layers, were always there. He seemed to live far back in the cave of his mind, emotionless except at rare times, peeping out at the world like some sly, concealed hermit. Only when he was angered did his emotions come rushing forth from the cavern's mouth like a swarm of dark bats.

When I was a young boy, I often hated him, hated the endless chores, the stinking rows of cotton, the patched hand-me-downs that marked us as sharecroppers—"poor white trash" living from hand to mouth and moving from pillar to post. Not until I was past forty did I begin to have a glimmering of what he and Mom went through, raising four kids in nearly impossible circumstance. I stopped feeling I'd had a lousy childhood then and started being grateful.

It was an odd twist of fate that made Dad a rich man's kid—only to take away his parents and make him poor. Once his older brothers and his father had toasted each successful crop—money in the bank—and the upcoming hog drive to the railhead at Wichita Falls. They herded the grunting porkers across the Red River like cattle drives of old. That all stopped when George E. Rastus died.

Dad will take a lifetime of events, adventures, and memories to his final rest. No matter how I, the family chronicler, try to trick him, there are some things he will not tell me, perhaps because they're just too painful.

Yet sometimes he's remarkably candid about very personal things. Once on a hot summer's day as we stood in the hay field, this silent, reserved man said quietly, "Reckon I oughta tell you somethin'. You ain't my kid, but I always loved you just as much as the others."

I turned away, looking toward a great white cloud, a finger pointing toward heaven. "Yeah, I know," I said, choking a little because I handle such stuff poorly. "How you think I put up with you all those years?"

There are seven graves in the Childress plot in the old Navaho Cemetery west of Cache, Oklahoma. But the main ones are the graves of George E. Rastus Childress, Sudie Childress, and Infant Childress, who lies between them.

Someday Dad will be there, too. But the words he spoke to me in the hay field that day will live on, my legacy from a man whose childhood ought to have rendered him powerless to love—yet who somehow was able to utter a sentence I'll always remember.

※ ※ ※

There is a blitheness in the Ozarks, a taking-for-granted that is partly human nature and partly the endless details of daily living. The days turn inward on themselves like dying earthworms, and long intervals pass with nothing happening.

And then, suddenly, someone's life comes to an end in an Ozark accident or because of illness. Where form and substance once was, we now grow used to empty space. Whatever humans finally are, whatever their trials and victories, whatever impact they made on those around them, it all stops when they stop.

And so it was as last year drew to a close. We are used to Christmas deaths here—we know from past experience that death loves a holiday. Sometimes, too, death loves irony.

December 29 dawned cold, gray, and orange. The cold and the gray were the fog that wrapped Route F. The orange was the flames leaping upward from Paul Marshall's farmhouse.

Few things galvanize neighbors like a rural fire. The nearest fire trucks are in Anderson, six miles away. At 6:30, the Marshalls lay sleeping in their bedroom. The home had no rear escape door. On the couch, a milker's helper, twenty-four-year-old Terry Rudd, also slept. He awoke to flames and smoke billowing from the utility room and aroused the Marshalls.

Trapped by the fire, the three ran into a bedroom and broke the window. The ground lay six feet down. Squirming through, the Marshalls were severely gashed, with Paul Marshall's cuts later requiring sixty stitches.

Rudd did not come out behind them, so Marshall bravely went back in, finding the milker unconscious from smoke. But Marshall, a slightly-built man, could not raise the dead weight to the window. Meanwhile, Mrs. Marshall had run a quarter mile to the home of a neighbor, Darrel Sanders. He and his son, Marty, a McDonald County High School senior, returned to the Marshall home—now engulfed in flames.

Young Sanders courageously crawled back into the burning house, but at first Rudd couldn't be found. He had regained consciousness and, dazed, had tried to find another exit—and fallen between a bed and the wall. Marty Sanders crawled along a hallway until he found Rudd, and despite flames and heavy smoke, dragged the man to the window, pushed him through, and saved his life.

By now, neighbors had seen the flames through the low-lying haze, and rushed to help. Melvin Carnes, a chicken farmer, was among them. But it was too late to save much of anything. As the Elk River Ambulance Service took away the bleeding Marshalls, two Anderson fire trucks completed the six-mile journey from town.

"There was a time when we thought we could save some of it," said volunteer fireman Gene Hall. "But then we ran out of water."

No hydrants exist on rural routes, so fire trucks siphon water from livestock ponds. In doing so, the trucks bogged down, and by the time they returned with full tanks, the fire had done its work.

One by one, as firemen mopped up, neighbors drifted homeward—among them Melvin Carnes. Life went on. He had to awaken his hired hand, thirty-year-old David Hines, who slept in a small trailer behind the house, and who usually went away for weekends.

"I knocked on the door," Carnes said afterward. "There was no answer, so I figured maybe he'd quit, and I called his dad to see. But his dad hadn't seen him either. He and his son came down, and lacking a key, took the door off the camping trailer David batched in."

Inside, David Hines and his dog lay dead, victims of asphyxiation. On the propane stove, a single burner glowed. In the gloom, it looked like the solitary, star-splintered light that graces Christmas trees.

❧ ❧ ❧

When I was a kid on a sharecrop farm in the 1940s, there were no noisy celebrations—at least not on the level of those in the larger cities. But that was only because we were too tired—for work on the farm never stops. Cows must be milked and livestock fed on New Year's Eve the same as any other day. So, in a sense, the phrase "New Year's" didn't exist for us. We knew the holiday mainly as a changing of numbers.

But there was an aura about the season, a halo of hope that this time the numbers would come up positive. Sharecroppers didn't have a lot of good years, but there were some. For Dad, worried about the bills, there was the hope that he had enough seed corn or wheat and that all the livestock would pull through the winter—for on January 1, the worst still lay ahead.

Christmas was, for us, the major holiday of the year, but there were some isolated New Year's celebrations—and we made the most of them.

For instance, we always had a fine New Year's dinner. Of course the feasting was royal—pies, cakes, perhaps a roast duck, especially if duck season had been good to us. And for the grown-ups, there was a rural version of the wassail bowl—also known as "native corn," "white lightnin'," or "moonshine." It was illegal, but it was our way of thumbing our noses at the politicians who made some strange laws anyway—and who, past experience had shown, cared not too much about the plight of rural families.

I used to wonder about that, until one day Dad enlightened me.

"We live under a system of one man, one vote," he told me. "In the big cities, there's just a lot more folks than there are on the farm—so the politicians tend to pay more attention to the cities."

He said it without rancor. It was simply a fact of rural life. On the other hand, every time a new year turned, we rustics thanked our stars because we lived without traffic, fumes, noise, or much crime. So it all balanced out, we felt.

On the Oklahoma Plains, January rarely came without bringing a snow—often a huge blizzard of awesome beauty, blanketing the yellow rangeland with virginal whiteness. Nothing could make us see the changing of the year like new-fallen snow. At night, when coyotes performed symphonies under the stars, there was such an air of peace and isolation that our family celebration took on an almost religious air. It was as if we performed our tiny duties on a great white stage— and our only audience was the angels.

One New Year's Day is still vivid in my memory. I rose exactly at sunrise—late for me—and walked outside to a scene of unbelievable beauty. The red yolk of the sun cast its low rays across snow that had crystallized into ice on top. This frostlike crust glittered like acres of diamonds—or, where trees cut the light into pieces, like red rubies and opals flecked with a shimmering translucence.

On New Year's Eve, we children were allowed to stay up extra late—even though the next day would have its full complement of chores that had to be done. We didn't mind. It was fun to huddle on the floor around our old battery-powered Philco, listening to special comedy programs and, very late at night, to a new guy named Lombardo whose band was fast becoming a New Year's tradition.

How curious it is to look back and recall the primitive lives we led—at a time when atomic power and jet planes had not been invented. We had no electricity other than the few volts our cranky old wind-charger gave us, though a few of the richer farmers had home generators. Eventually, of course, the power company discovered us. They planted poles in the ground, strung their lines and, somehow, things were no longer the same.

New Year's was also a time for long-distance telephone calls. We didn't have a telephone, but Mom would go down the road to a neighbor's and get on the wall-crank phone, wait for an operator, then hang up the phone and visit for upwards of an hour while the call to West Coast kinfolks crept through. It was a visit shared via party-line with any others who had telephones, too.

And so we lived each year in hard work and hope—hope for a better future and for continuing peace in those years between wars. We made the most of every hour of leisure, for they were p ecious few. Nor did we ever complain about our jobs, for we were almighty glad to be working, to be making a living. The terrors of the Great Depression were still vivid in all our minds.

We found much to be grateful for, even in the face of adversity. Rural living will do that for you with its livestock ponds jeweled in ice (we made rude skis of barrel-staves and slid or tumbled down the pond dams) and with spring more than a promise, even as snow hurled by winds rattled against the walls of a sharecrop shack.

"Hope," the wind seemed to say. "Hope."

And so we did. Even as the strains of *Auld Lang Syne* drifted from the radio, we hoped that the year just being born would be better than the very best year we had ever known.

Epilogue

My sun is poised at noon,
relentless to begin
its final arc.
Winds are eroding me
that blinded Cleopatra
and gave Anthony to the dark.

The dusty hours flow
through corridors of glass
that ushered Tutankhamen
and framed Pavlova's grace.
With dancer and with Pharaoh,
I share all we hold common.

I sink into the sands
that smothered mighty Caesar;
that packed the tomb of Christ
and measured Mary's bed.
Each day the span decreases
from the living to the dead.

Sometimes there is such beauty in the southwestern Missouri Ozarks that I stop what I am doing and simply stare. I am a stranger at the portals of heaven, and no potion or drug can enrich my vision.

One recent evening, just as dusk was turning to darkness, a final reflection of the vanished sun ricocheted off a golden cloud bank—and the pastures were transformed. I'd been driving up the lane. I stopped.

A soft, late breeze slithered across the pasture grass (higher this year than I can ever remember it because of heavy rains). The wind made the fields change color, from deepest amber to brightest gold and back again—as though some hidden army held the edges of a great carpet and shook it on command.

I can no more define my feelings than I can fly—but every year I live here makes it harder for me to leave. People do leave the Ozarks, of course—and some have come with high hopes of finding the simple life, though I think there is no simple life anymore, and perhaps there never was. It is only time's web of years that makes us see the past as brightly as the sea of grass I gazed upon.

The amber waves caused by the ever-lessening breeze began to be lost in darkness. It was a mood of such solitude and loneliness, no poet on earth could do it justice. Yet such moments sustain me, mellow me, make a day that might have soured with the morning news as sweet as fresh milk.

Oh, beautiful, far-spacious fields . . .

The sky was putting on one final splendor. A storm had been slowly building, and the northwestern horizon's blackness had merged with the coming night. But out of it a bronze cornucopia of light opened and poured a final blessing on the fields. Jagged stalks of lightning filigreed the clouds, a jewelry no one could wear. The wind, so soft and summery before, turned cold and cutting. The grass bent almost flat. The moon still hid below the eastern skyline. The storm struck just as I turned into my gullied driveway, and even from forty feet away the fury of the rain almost hid my house. A race to the door drenched me as completely as if I'd fallen into a river. But I love Ozark storms, and often stand out in them, shouting at the pouring rain and raging wind like some bearded Old Man of the Mountains. At such times I feel equal to the elements, a forest god who, with proper obeisance towards Olympus, could live in the Ozarks a thousand times ten thousand years.

And never grow tired of it.

The son of migrant workers, William Childress has degrees from Fresno State College and from the University of Iowa's famed Writer's Workshop. He has published in periodicals ranging from *Family Circle* and *Harper's* to *Poetry* (Chicago) and the *New Republic*. Mr. Childress has written regular columns for *Sports Afield* and other magazines; his column in *Friends,* the Chevrolet magazine, is in its eighth year. His current column in the *St. Louis Post-Dispatch* has twice been nominated for the Pulitzer Prize. Between public appearances, Mr. Childress lives in a walnut grove, where he sometimes pretends he is Bill Monroe, "the greatest mandolinist in the universe."